160 415751 7

D1338223

wo week
oan

Please return on or before the last
date stamped below.
Charges are made for late return.

23 FEB 1999
25 MAR 1999

WITHDRAWN

9 FEB 2000

01 FEB 2001

15 NOV 2001

19 N
19 NOV 2001

19 NOV 2001

CARDIFF UNIVERSITY LIBRARIES, PO BOX 430, CARDIFF CF1 3XT

F 114/0796

1-95

Central

e week loan

4 NOV 1994		

Key Concepts in Political Scienc

GENERAL EDITOR: Leonard B. Schapiro

EXECUTIVE EDITOR: Peter Calvert

Other titles in the same series include:

Anthony H. Birch	**Representation**
Peter Calvert	**Revolution**
Brian Chapman	**Police State**
Ioan Davies	**Social Mobility and Political Change**
Joseph Frankel	**National Interest**
C. J. Friedrich	**Tradition and Authority**
P. H. Partridge	**Consent and Consensus**
Otto Pick and Julian Critchley	**Collective Security**
John. Plamenatz	**Ideology**
John C. Rees	**Equality**
Leonard B. Schapiro	**Totalitarianism**
Henry Tudor	**Political Myth**
Paul Wilkinson	**Social Movement**

Bureaucracy

Martin Albrow
University College, Cardiff

M

UWIST
CARDIFF
library
18 DEC 1981
ACCESSION NUMBER 151529
CLASS NUMBER 301.1832

CARBS
Albrow

© 1970 by Pall Mall Press Ltd, Londo

All rights reserved. No part of this publication may b
reproduced or transmitted, in any form or by any mean
without permissio

First published in 1970 by Pall Mall Press Lt

This edition published in 1970 b
Macmillan and Company Limite
and reprinted in 1978, 1979 b
THE MACMILLAN PRESS LT
London and Basingstok
Associated companies in Delhi Dubli
Hong Kong Johannesburg Lagos Melbourn
New York Singapore and Toky

ISBN 0 333 11262

Printed in Hong Kon

Not for sale in the U.S.A

This book is sold subject to the standard conditio
of the Net Book Agreemen

The paperback edition of this book is sold subject
the condition that it shall not, by way of trade or otherwis
be lent, resold, hired out, or otherwise circulated without t
publisher's prior consent in any form of binding or cover oth
than that in which it is published and without a simil
condition including this condition being imposed on t
subsequent purchase

Contents

'Key Concepts'
an Introductory Note 7

Acknowledgements 11

Introduction 13

1/The Emergence of the Concept 16

ıe origin of the term 16
rly nineteenth-century concepts 18
ıe English theory 21
ntinental theory 26
ıe major nineteenth-century themes 30

2/The Classical Formulations 33

osca and Michels 33
ıx Weber: the theory of organization 37
ıx Weber: the concept of bureaucracy 40
ıx Weber: the limits on bureaucracy 45

3/The Debate with Weber 50

e sources of Weber's theory 50
e case against Weber 54
eply to the critics 61

4/Bureaucracy and the Ideologists 67

rl Marx 68
e later Marxists 72
e Fascists 79
e ideologists of representative democracy 81

5/Seven Modern Concepts of Bureaucracy

Bureaucracy as rational organization
Bureaucracy as organizational inefficiency
Bureaucracy as rule by officials
Bureaucracy as public administration
Bureaucracy as administration by officials
Bureaucracy as the organization
Bureaucracy as modern society

6/Bureaucracy and the Theorists of Democracy

The changing intellectual context
The diagnosis of bureaucracy
The remedies for bureaucracy

Conclusion: The Concept of Bureaucracy in Social and Political Science

Notes and References

Bibliography

Index

'Key Concepts' an Introductory Note

Political concepts are part of our daily speech—we abuse reaucracy' and praise 'democracy', welcome or recoil from volution'. Emotive words such as 'equality', 'dictatorship', te' or even 'power' can often, by the very passions which they e, obscure a proper understanding of the sense in which they , or should be, or should not be, or have been used. Confucius arded the 'rectification of names' as the first task of government. names are not correct, language will not be in accordance with truth of things', and this in time would lead to the end of ice, to anarchy and to war. One could with some truth point out t the attempts hitherto by governments to enforce their own int meanings on words have not been conspicuous for their suc- s in the advancement of justice. 'Rectification of names' there st certainly be: but most of us would prefer such rectification to e place in the free debate of the university, in the competitive na of the pages of the book or journal.

Analysis of commonly used political terms, their reassessment or ir 'rectification', is, of course, normal activity in the political ence departments of our universities. The idea of this series was eed born in the course of discussion between a few university chers of political science, of whom Professor S. E. Finer of nchester University was one. It occurred to us that a series of rt books, discussing the 'Key Concepts' in political science uld serve two purposes. In universities these books could pro- le the kind of brief political texts which might be of assistance to dents in gaining a fuller understanding of the terms which they re constantly using. But we also hoped that outside the univer- es there exists a reading public which has the time, the curiosity d the inclination to pause to reflect on some of those words and as which are so often taken for granted. Perhaps even 'that insidi- s and crafty animal', as Adam Smith described the politician and tesman, will occasionally derive some pleasure or even profit m that more leisurely analysis which academic study can afford, d which a busy life in the practice of politics often denies.

It has been very far from the minds of those who have been co cerned in planning and bringing into being the 'Key Concep series to try and impose (as if that were possible!) any unifo pattern on the authors who have contributed, or will contribute, it. I, for one, hope that each author will, in his own individ manner, seek and find the best way of helping us to a fuller und standing of the concept which he has chosen to analyse. But wh ever form the individual exposition may take, there are, I belie three aspects of illumination which we can confidently expect fr each volume in this series. First, we can look for some examinati of the history of the concept, and of its evolution against a changi social and political background. I believe, as many do who are co cerned with the study of political science, that it is primarily history that the explanation must be sought for many of the p plexing problems of political analysis and judgement which be us today. Second, there is the semantic aspect. To look in depth a 'key concept' necessarily entails a study of the name whi attached itself to it; of the different ways in which, and the differe purposes for which, the name was used; of the way in which in t course of history the same name was applied to several concepts, several names were applied to one and the same concept; and, i deed, of the changes which the same concept, or what appears be the same concept, has undergone in the course of time. Th analysis will usually require a searching examination of the rel vant literature in order to assess the present stage of scholarship each particular field. And thirdly, I hope that the reader of ea volume in this series will be able to decide for himself what t proper and valid use should be of a familiar term in politics, a will gain, as it were, from each volume a sharper and bette tempered tool of political analysis.

There are many today who would disagree with Bismarck's vi that politics can never be an exact science. I express no opinion this much debated question. But all of us who are students politics—and our numbers both inside and outside the universiti continue to grow—will be the better for knowing what precisely mean when we use a common political term.

London School of Economics
and Political Science

Leonard B. Schapi
General Edit

for my parents

Mouzelis
Bureaucracy

Warwick D (1974)
Bureaucracy

Acknowledgements

The following read various drafts of this book and mmented helpfully: Peter Calvert, University of South-npton; Professor S. E. Finer, University of Manchester; nthony Giddens, King's College, Cambridge; Helmuth eisler, University College, Cardiff; Michael Hill, Uni-rsity of Reading; Professor L. B. Schapiro, London hool of Economics; Paul Wilkinson, University College, rdiff. At the Pall Mall Press, Derick Mirfin provided valuable support and prompting and laboured manfully th the text. The staff of the British Museum, the itish Library of Political and Economic Science, and e Inter-Library Loan section of the library of Univer-y College, Cardiff have been unfailingly efficient. Sally brow has met all the importunate demands that an thor makes of his wife, as well as looking after three ildren. I am very grateful to all these people, and absolve em of any responsibility for what follows.

Cardiff
October 1, 1969

Martin C. Albrow

Introduction

On January 29, 1968 the British House of Commons de-
ted a Conservative motion condemning 'the continued growth of
reaucracy'. At the same time the motion deplored the failure of
e Labour government to announce 'clear proposals to streamline
e machinery of government and so to reduce the numbers em-
oyed in the public service'.[1] For most of the debate the two issues
re treated as identical. But one member did express his dis-
pointment that there was no discussion of more general ideas,
d that 'bureaucracy' was being measured merely in numbers. He
ggested that its essence was that 'the people who are appointed
e not responsible to the people whose lives they affect'.[2] When a
bsequent speaker tried to develop this argument he was told that
was not about the quality of government that they were debating
t simply about the number of civil servants. He retorted that the
ords "continued growth of bureaucracy" imply a sneer'.[3] For
n talk of bureaucracy raised more issues than the question of the
e of the civil service.

It would be wrong to attribute these semantic difficulties to a
cline in the capacity of British politicians to communicate with
ch other. In political debate, whether in the context of Stansted
Crichel Down, Medicare or the New Deal, and going back long
fore those controversies, 'bureaucracy' has been a term of strong
otive overtones and elusive connotations.

Those who turn to social and political science in the hope of find-
g illumination of this concept can only be disappointed. Political
entists, sociologists, management scientists have all devoted
jor pieces of theory and research to bureaucracy. The result of
s academic division of labour has been a proliferation of con-
ots. In the search for terminological precision agreement on the
ncept has receded to the point where specialists in these neigh-
uring disciplines tolerate the existence of completely incom-
tible concepts of bureaucracy without comment. But, in spite of

prefacing their work with remarks such as: 'bureaucracy elud definition';[4] or 'the term bureaucracy is devoid of any establishe meaning',[5] writers have gone on to discuss bureaucracy, whatev it may be. For social and political scientists are as much in agre ment that 'the problems of bureaucracy' are important for academ thought and research, as politicians and the public are that th are worth debate.

The student coming to this field can be excused bewildermen Sometimes 'bureaucracy' seems to mean administrative efficienc at other times the opposite. It may appear as simple as a synony for civil service, or it may be as complex as an idea summing up t specific features of modern organizational structure. It may refer a body of officials, or to the routines of office administration.

This book is offered in aid of a clarification of this situation. does not aim to set up a new theory of bureaucracy, nor even a ne concept. (The reader will meet theories and concepts enough in t ensuing pages to make him welcome this act of self-abnegation c the part of the writer.) Nor is its aim to act as arbiter between t competing concepts, to label one or other as 'authoritative'. T task is conceived of as one of exposition: examining the wide var ety of concepts of bureaucracy, investigating their relations, an explaining their development. In consequence 'bureaucracy' is a ways used in the text as reported speech, and never to refer to concept of the writer's own.

It is hoped that this stock-taking will be useful at several level While the objective throughout has been to make the concept bureaucracy intelligible to the newcomer to the subject, as so ofte happens with such exercises the author has been forced, in purs ing that purpose, to present new material. The modern concern f the logic of concept-formation has not been accompanied by a equal emphasis on the temporal and contextual limitations on t process of forming concepts in social science. The fact that t concept of bureaucracy has a history has been forgotten. The fir chapter attempts to remedy this by showing how some of the mo puzzling contradictions in modern concepts of bureaucracy arise nineteenth-century theories. Partly as a consequence of this, t interpretation of Max Weber's concept of bureaucracy that offered here differs markedly from recent accounts of this aspect his work.

The same specialization which has involved the neglect of t

igins of its concepts has given rise to genres of writing on bureau-
acy quite isolated from each other. In consequence the modest
ɔjective of this book—to examine what is meant by those who
rite of bureaucracy—necessitates an immodest coverage of com-
eting concepts in different disciplines. But the author believes
at the novice has something to gain from this, and that the speci-
ist who finds some part of the final chapters entirely familiar can
ill benefit from finding, juxtaposed to it, material from another
ɔecialty. In this last respect it is hoped that the bibliography will
e a useful supplement to older and more general compilations by
Merton and Eisenstadt.[6]

Although no attempt is made to produce a definitive concept of
ureaucracy, the account in this book does seem to suggest some
eneral conclusions on *desiderata* for any future conceptualizations
this field. The final chapter offers some suggestions for the allevi-
ion of the present confusion on the basis of a brief consideration
f some of the issues of concept-formation in social science that are
ised in writing on bureaucracy. But such relief is more to be
ought in a consciousness of the development and logical affiliations
f the different concepts of bureaucracy. The author hopes that the
emedy may be found in the analysis itself.

1 / The Emergence of the Concept

The origin of the term

In a letter of July 1, 1764, the Baron de Grimm, the Frenc philosopher, wrote: 'We are obsessed by the idea of regulation, ar our Masters of Requests refuse to understand that there is a infinity of things in a great state with which a government shoul not concern itself. The late M. de Gournay[1] . . . sometimes used t say: "We have an illness in France which bids fair to play havc with us; this illness is called bureaumania". Sometimes he used t invent a fourth or fifth form of government under the heading c bureaucracy.'[2] A year later the same author wrote: 'The real spir of the laws of France is that bureaucracy of which the late M. d Gournay . . . used to complain so greatly; here the offices, clerk secretaries, inspectors and *intendants* are not appointed to benef the public interest, indeed the public interest appears to have bee established so that offices might exist.'[3]

We are fortunate in having the invention of the word so precisel documented.[4] But it would be a mistake to confuse the coining of term with the revelation of a new concept. Since de Gournay a ver wide variety of ideas has been brought together under the headin of bureaucracy. Many have origins too remote to trace. Complaint about bad government must be as old as government itself. Con cern that sovereigns should be served by diligent and faithfu officials was a commonplace in political thought long before th eighteenth century. Machiavelli urged the prince to choose com petent ministers, and to reward their fidelity so that they shoul not have to seek rewards from other sources.[5] Not even the idea c administrative efficiency is peculiar to modern, or indeed Wester thought. From 165 B.C. Chinese officials were selected by examina tion. Chinese administration was familiar with notions of seniority merit ratings, official statistics and written reports and the writin of Shen Pu-hai (d. 337 B.C.) provided a set of principles whic have been likened to twentieth-century theories of administration.

Such ideas about government did not have to wait upon d

ournay's flair for expression before they could be expressed. But ere are two reasons why his formulation should be regarded as gnificant. He explicitly evokes the classical Greek classification of overnments. In so doing he invents another type of government add to long recognized forms, such as monarchy, aristocracy d democracy. He does not, therefore, conceive of eighteenth-ntury French government as some malformation of monarchy, ch as tyranny. He is identifying a new group of rulers and a ethod of governing. The complaint against them is not that they e acting unlawfully, outside their proper authority, but that overning seems to have become an end in itself. This addition to e classical typology, albeit cursorily identified, must be regarded an important conceptual innovation.

The second reason for emphasizing de Gournay's invention is lated to the first, but is almost adventitious. It concerns the popu-rity the term has acquired. In the language of the eighteenth ntury 'bureau', as well as signifying a writing-table, already eant a place where officials worked. The addition of a suffix, erived from the Greek word for 'rule', resulted in a term with onsiderable power to penetrate other cultures. The Greek con-epts of government had long been domesticated in the major uropean languages. The new term could easily undergo the same ansliterations as 'democracy' or 'aristocracy'. It rapidly became art of an international vocabulary of politics. The French *bureau-atie* rapidly became the German *Bureaukratie* (later *Bürokratie*), e Italian *burocrazia*, and the English 'bureaucracy'. Further-ore, on analogy with the derivatives of democracy, with bureau-racy went bureaucrat, bureaucratic, bureaucratism, bureaucratist nd bureaucratization.

It is, therefore, not surprising that early dictionary definitions of ureaucracy are highly consistent, both with each other and with e Gournay. The Dictionary of the French Academy accepted the ord in its 1798 supplement and defined it as: 'Power, influence of e heads and staff of governmental bureaux.'[7] An 1813 edition of German dictionary of foreign expressions defined bureaucracy s: 'The authority or power which various government departments nd their branches arrogate to themselves over fellow citizens.'[8] n Italian technical dictionary of 1828 referred to it thus: 'Neo-ogism, signifying the power of officials in public administration.'[9] he French Academy also accepted 'bureaucratic' in reference to 'the influence of governmental bureaux, and also a regime whe bureaux multiply without need'. This dual meaning attributed 'bureaucratic' gives the first hint of the complex development t concept was to undergo.

Early nineteenth-century concepts

In spite of its origins in the thinking of the French physi crats and its acceptance by the lexicographers, the early use of t term 'bureaucracy' seems to have been confined to the works polemicists and novelists. Balzac was largely responsible for pop larizing the word in French. His novel of 1836, *Les Employés*, w actually half treatise on the ways of bureaucracy. His vituperati tone is a good example of a way of thinking that has never cease to have its adherents:

> Since 1789 the State, or if you like to have it so, *La Patr* has taken the place of the sovereign. The clerks no long take their instructions directly from one of the first magi trates in the realm . . . and thus Bureaucracy, the gia power wielded by pigmies, came into the world. Possib Napoleon retarded its influence for a time, for all things ar all men were forced to bend to his will. . . . Bureaucra was definitely organized, however, under a constitution government with a natural kindness for mediocrity, a pred lection for categorical statements and reports, a governme as fussy and meddlesome, in short, as a small shopkeeper wife.[10]

So successful was Balzac in projecting his image of burea cracy that when Le Play attempted the first serious French co sideration of the concept in 1864, he felt obliged to apologize f 'this hybrid word created by a light literature'.[11] The 1873 editic of Littré's dictionary still felt that the word was a barely corre neologism.[12] Even in 1896 a French political dictionary expresse the view that the word originated in Germany and was on popularized in France by Balzac.[13]

The idea that the term came from Germany was not surprisin During the French Revolution German newspapers reported even in France and spoke of bureaucracy without further explanation. Outside the press the earliest known German reference to burea cracy would appear to be by Christian Kraus, one of Kant lleagues. In a letter of 1799 he contrasted Prussia with England, ıere, he argued, the populace remained the rock-fast base of the ramid of state, while 'the Prussian state, far from being an unıited monarchy . . . is but a thinly veiled aristocracy, . . . which ıtantly rules the country as a bureaucracy'.[15] The term, however, i not immediately enter serious political writing. Wilhelm von ımboldt's essay of 1792, *An Attempt to Determine the Limits of Effectiveness of the State*, failed to mention bureaucracy. But its eme, the fear that an increase of state authority entailed the owth of administration, and the fear that the affairs of state were coming mechanical while men were being transformed into achines, was later to become commonplace in polemics against ıreaucracy.[16]

Humboldt's fears were echoed in a letter of the Freiherr vom ein in 1821. Stein did not shrink from indicting the system he d administered and reformed after the Prussian defeat by apoleon in 1806. But he spoke of *Büralisten* rather than ıreaucrats:

> We are ruled by buralists—salaried, with a knowledge of books, with no cause to support, and without property. . . . In these four points is summed up the spirit of our own and similar lifeless governmental machines: salaried, hence striving to maintain and increase the number of those with salaries; with a knowledge of books, hence not living in the real world, but in one of letters; with no cause to support, for they are allied with none of the classes of citizens that constitute the state, they are a caste in their own right, the caste of clerks, without property, and therefore unaffected by its fluctuations. Come rain or sunshine, whether taxes rise or fall, whether long-established rights are destroyed or preserved, it makes no difference to them. They draw their salaries from the exchequer and write, write, write, in silence, in offices behind closed doors, unknown, unnoticed, unpraised, and they bring up their children to be equally usable writing machines.[17]

This passage was used by Karl Heinzen, a radical who had flee from Prussia. He included it in his polemic of 1845 against russian bureaucracy, but he substituted 'bureaucrat' for 'buralist' s well as adding embellishments of his own).[18]

Probably the work of Johan Görres did most to publicize t concept of bureaucracy in early nineteenth-century Germa Publicist, romantic, founder of the newspaper the *Rheinisc Merkur*, he became so important an opponent of the monarc that he also was forced to leave Prussia. Using the classical typolo of government to provide the elements of his analysis he develop a theory of the basis of national unity. Monarchical and democra elements had to be combined to provide co-operation and mut respect between rulers and ruled. Bureaucracy was the result wh these conditions were not fulfilled. In *Europe and the Revolut* (1821), he saw bureaucracy as the civil institution analogous to t standing army. It was based on the same principles of discipli promotion, group honour and centralization. The administrati techniques which filled the gap left by the lack of trust betwe rulers and ruled became principles of state. Bureaucracy succeed 'in extending the principle of subordination, which was basic to own development, from its own organism to the subject popu tion, to conglomerate them gradually into masses, in which peo only counted as numbers, deriving value not from their selves, b from their positions'.[19]

It is important to note a dual emphasis in these early ideas bureaucracy. It is viewed not only as a form of government whe power is in the hands of officials; it is also a collective designati for those officials. If one considers the concepts of aristocracy a democracy it is possible to see how this could have happene 'Aristocracy' is used almost exclusively to refer to a particu social stratum, rather than to a form of government. On the oth hand 'democracy' is normally taken to refer to the institutio forms through which the will of a population may be realize (This is a long way, incidentally, from the Aristotelian concept democracy as the rule of a class.) Either emphasis was possible the early conceptualizations of bureaucracy. The early writers the subject perceived clearly that this new form of government w related to a new element in the system of social stratification. It c not seem inappropriate, given the use of the term 'aristocracy', refer to that new element as 'the bureaucracy'.

In English syntax the presence or absence of an article norma signifies which of the two aspects of the concept is being stress 'the' or 'a bureaucracy' referring to a body of bureaucrats; 'burea cracy' designating procedures of administration. In more rec gon, the concept of bureaucracy has comprised both institutional d associational aspects. On this simple, but vital, distinction pend two basic modes of sociological thinking: the analysis of ion, and the analysis of groups. If this distinction had always en recognized much of the confusion in the literature on bureaucy could have been avoided.

The English theory

It is largely through translations from the German literae that we are able to determine the time of the reception of reaucracy' into English. An earlier work by Görres, *Germany d the Revolution* (1819), was translated into English in two separ- versions in 1820.[20] In both cases direct translation of *bureautisch* into 'bureaucratic' was avoided.[21] On the other hand an 32 translation of the travel letters of a German prince reported view thus: 'The Bureaucracy has taken the place of the Aristocy, and will perhaps soon become equally hereditary.'[22] The 27 edition of Johnson's *Dictionary* had no entry for the word. the other hand *The Popular Encyclopaedia* of 1837 (itself based the great German *Conversationslexicon*), contained an item on 'bureau system, or bureaucracy'.[23]

These translations encouraged a contrast to be drawn between gland and the Continent which became a standard part of nineth-century observations on bureaucracy. In the great periodis, such as *Blackwood's* or the *Westminster Review*, commentary continental institutions almost invariably included a self-ngratulatory rider on how different things were in England. rlyle's terse comment in 1850 on bureaucracy—'the continental isance . . . I can see no risk or possibility in England. Democracy not enough here . . .'—summed up the prevailing English judgent on the subject.[24] Even Herbert Spencer, who was so conned to establish the limits and functions of the state, was content mention bureaucracy in the context of comments on France.[25] wever it should not be thought that the assessments of bureacy in the nineteenth-century journals were invariably as perctory as Carlyle's. Many of them anticipated points upon which ole theories have been centred. An essay of 1836 on the French ucational system observed that, for any defect in bureaucratic chinery, the remedy always took the form of further machin-.[26] In 1842 J. S. Blackie, a commentator on the German scene, considered that the way in which the Prussian bureaucracy monc olized the intelligence of the nation was detrimental to energy a enterprise outside it, and resulted in submissiveness and servilit

This last point was one which particularly impressed the ma English writer on bureaucracy in the nineteenth century, Jc Stuart Mill. In his *Principles of Political Economy* (1848), he himself against 'concentrating in a dominant bureaucracy all skill and experience in the management of large interests, and the power of organized action, existing in the community'. He s it as 'a main cause of the inferior capacity for political life wh has hitherto characterized the over-governed countries of continent'.[28]

In *On Liberty* (1859), Mill developed these views still furth The dangers of bureaucracy were singled out for the peroration that immensely influential essay. He held them to constitute third and most important reason for objecting to government int ference, even when it did not infringe liberty. For, the more fu tions a government took on the more careers it offered, and th the more hangers-on it attracted. The more efficient the machin of administration, the more it would monopolize the talent of nation. To be admitted to the bureaucracy would be the sum of ambition, while outside it there would be few qualified criticize. Both governors and governed become the slaves of bureaucracy, and no reform would be possible. 'Where everythi is done through the bureaucracy, nothing to which the bureaucr is really adverse can be done at all.'[29]

The concept of bureaucracy reached its full importance in Mi political theory in his *Considerations on Representative Governm* (1861). In comparing types of government, he argued that the o form, other than the representative, which had high political s and ability was bureaucracy, even when it went under the name a monarchy or aristocracy. 'The work of government has been the hands of governors by profession; which is the essence a meaning of bureaucracy.'[30] Such a government 'accumulates perience, acquires well-tried and well-considered traditio maxims, and makes provision for appropriate practical knowle in those who have the actual conduct of affairs'.[31] But, on the de side, bureaucracies die of routine. 'They perish by the immu bility of their maxims.'[32] Only the popular element in governm was capable of allowing the conceptions of a man of original gen revail over trained mediocrity. The governments of China and sia were examples of what happened when the bureaucracy l power. Skined administration was certainly necessary, but it to be under the general control of bodies representative of the ole people.[33]

Mill's formulations were brief but influential. The sharp anti- ay he discerned between bureaucracy and democracy has been nined repeatedly since his writing. But just as important as the stantive issue of the relations of the administrative system to stitutional democracy—which his concept of bureaucracy alighted—was the analytical issue of what criteria were appro- te for classifying governments. Mill's emphasis, in contrasting aocracy and bureaucracy, was on the locus of decision-making real power, not upon the formal processes of selection for posedly sovereign bodies. This was of great importance in oing Mosca's ideas (see chapter 2), and, more immediately, ved a very suitable theme for more concrete elaboration by the t incisive nineteenth-century commentator on the English stitution, Walter Bagehot.

n *The English Constitution* (1867), Bagehot warned against any ue admiration for the Prussian state system that might be asioned by its recent military successes. The successes of bur- cracy could only be limited. It depended on routine which, pted to one situation, was insufficiently flexible to meet new oblems. Only sixty years before the Prussian system was held e 'dead and formal'. In fact Bagehot was less impressed than l with the efficiency of bureaucracy. 'The truth is that a skilled eaucracy—a bureaucracy trained from early life to its special cation—is, though it boasts the appearance of science, quite nsistent with the true principles of the art of business.'[34] This ot to say that Bagehot was against expertise, of the proper kind in the right place. He did not approve of the American system wholesale administrative changes when a new party came to er. (He was writing before the reforms made by President veland.) He indicted the classes from whose ranks English inistrators were drawn for ignorance and lack of business edu- on. He found the arrangement of public offices in England to casual and unsystematic.

ut, in spite of these defects, for Bagehot the great virtue of glish administration was that a frequent change of ministers never allowed it to sink into routine. New men, sensitive to outs opinion, were always available to re-invigorate the administra process. Bagehot was contrasting bureaucracy, unchecked by wi experience and opinion, with public administration in a systen parliamentary government. But he did not make use of M abstract justification that efficiency had to be tempered in the terests of liberty. Public administration in a democracy was actu more efficient. He likened it to the success of the great joint-st banks, the success of which depended 'on a due mixture of spe and non-special minds—of minds which attend to the means, of minds which attend to the end'.[35] This contrast between busin efficiency and bureaucracy was to become a standard one in work of twentieth-century conservative ideologists (see chapter

It would be wrong to suppose that the high opinion Englishn had of their own administrative system was simply a reflection insularity or jingoism. It was a view shared by very many cor nental scholars. From the standpoint of a political science (*Staa wissenschaft*) based in universities, German writers attempted describe the contrast between continental bureaucracy and Engl administration in precise terms. Eduard Fischel's *Die Verfass Englands* (1862) attempted to draw a lesson for German statesm from the English experience of self-government. In German d trine the unity of the state could not be secured without central ation. The high degree of autonomy enjoyed by the English gen in local government was unthinkable. But, argued Fischel, it v a mistake to think that centralization and self-government w incompatible. Without the hierarchy and authoritarianism t characterized Germany, English local government observed bc the common law and the wishes of parliament. The real inco patibility was between bureaucracy and self-government.[36]

Both the greater climate of freedom in England and the grea sophistication of continental political analysis would appear to confirmed by the fact that what is probably the first empiri study of bureaucracy was written by an Austrian for the *Conte porary Review* in 1880. Friedrich von Schulte's "Bureaucracy a its Operation in Germany and Austria-Hungary" repeated Fische argument that the Germans regarded self-government as a dir weakening of both crown and bureaucracy. In Germany there w 'a many-sided antithesis between the bureaucratic class and citiz class'.[37] But 'the tumour of bureaucracy',[38] had taken too deep

l. 'Everybody blames the Bureaucracy and asks from it every-
g he needs.'[39] Much in Schulte's analysis anticipates the
blem-settings of modern sociology. He set himself the task of
ewing 'the organization of the hierarchy of officials in its grada-
, titles, etc.; their pecuniary position; the cost of the public
inistration; the admission of non-officials into the hierarchical
r and society; the relation of the bureaucracy to self-govern-
t'.[40] In addition he compared the proportion of officials to
eral population in each of the major German states.

'owards the end of the century the self-confidence of English
ers on bureaucracy began to diminish. The reforms of the civil
ice, notably those of 1870, took it nearer to, rather than further
n, the continental services. In a speech in 1884 Sir Stafford
thcote, who had himself played an important part in the incep-
of these reforms, spoke of the dangers of a bureaucratic
potism in which 'the permanent officials will take the manage-
t of affairs into their hands, and Parliament will have little to
[41] No longer could bureaucracy be regarded as a foreign form
overnment. The danger was nearer home, and attacks on it
me increasingly strident.

the same year as Northcote's speech Herbert Spencer pub-
d a vehement attack on state intervention. In four essays in
Contemporary Review he castigated the Liberals for espousing
intervention and departing from their earlier concern for free-
of contract.[42] He detected a development analogous to that
rienced under continental bureaucracies. 'Increasing power of
owing administrative organization is accompanied by decreas-
power of the rest of society to resist its further growth and
rol. The multiplicity of careers opened by a developing bur-
racy tempts members of the classes regulated by it to favour
xtension, as adding to the chances of safe and respectable places
heir relatives.'[43]

lso in 1884, F. C. Montague's *The Limits of Individual Liberty*
eloped the same theme. On the Continent men had to acquiesce
regulated servitude. But there was no need to regard this as
itable in England. An employed bureaucracy regularly became
verning bureaucracy, inflexible, fond of power, but enslaved
routine. By accustoming men to heavy taxation and paternal
it 'stimulates all tendencies to communism'.[44] But in England,
iament, the courts and municipal liberties ensured that

administration and the community were identified, and bure
racy prevented. By the turn of the century it was recognized
bureaucracy had already arrived. One writer even argued that a
tion for female suffrage was simply an irrelevance, diverting at
tion from the real problem of bureaucratic government.[45] Bu
late as 1914, it was still possible to insist that the phenomenon,
the word, was an intrusion from abroad and not yet deeply ro
in British government.[46]

The English nineteenth-century theory of bureaucracy was
lucidly summarized in the historian Ramsay Muir's essay of
"Bureaucracy in England". For him bureaucracy meant 'the e
cise of power by professionalized administrators'.[47] 'The
steady, persistent and powerful influences in the governmen
England are those of the great permanent officials.'[48] But the
that it was 'essentially un-English' and a growth of the last
years, he criticized strongly. For more than seventy years it
been growing steadily. There had been 'the most astonishing
spiracy of silence to maintain this illusion' that the English sys
was non-bureaucratic.[49]

Muir's dismissal of the English belief in their freedom f
bureaucracy was an early expression of twentieth-century p
mism on this subject. Certainly this belief, illusion or not, and
English writing on this theme, of which it was a part, have lar
been forgotten. But its image of a society not governed by offi
was a major influence on the much more developed and profo
continental writing, which will be discussed in the remainde
this chapter and the next.

Continental theory

The contrast between English and German writing
bureaucracy was immense. The English writers feeling safely
tant from the continental type of government, did not hav
concern themselves with the technical minutiae of its operat
In their broad comparative perspective all European countries
of the same type: places where officials ruled. In any classifica
of governments bureaucracy had to appear as a major, and fo
nately foreign, variety. The English system of administration
not demand technical text books on, or degrees in, a science of
state, and criticism of this system did not have direct repercussi
on the personal liberty of the writer. The highly centralized Gerr

es were governed by professional officials, working on the is of official doctrines on administration. Hence writing on the ne of bureaucracy was either technical and an adjunct to legal nce, or it was an opposition literature, regarded by the state as versive. Lorenz von Stein, author of the great treatise on man administrative theory, tried, with unconscious humour, to the best possible complexion on this contrast. 'It is true that the nch and the English, whom we always regard as models, have her the concept nor the system of the State. But it is also true t they have absolutely no science of the State. This is precisely it puts the German genius so high above that of other nations, t we are striving to possess such a science.'[50]

t is vital for the understanding of the work of Max Weber cussed in the next chapter), that the contrasting *contexts* of rman and English writing on bureaucracy are recognized. In rmany the idea of bureaucracy was intimately connected with ical changes in both the theory and practice of administration owing the Prussian defeat by Napoleon in 1806. It would be long a task to pursue German administrative theory back into eighteenth century and further.[51] But, to characterize it briefly, vas dominated by the concept of the *collegium*, a body of officials rged with advising the ruler and taking responsibility for a parlar function of government, such as finance or law and order. is responsibility was a collective one, and there was considerable pe within the *collegium* for the clash of ideas and interests. After 6 the collegial system was replaced by what was called the *reau-* or *Einheitssystem*, in which responsibility was clearly vested n individual at each level of authority up to a minister.

The difference between the two systems was examined at length reatises on administration.[52] The collegial form had the advanes of subjecting decisions to discussion from many points of w. It developed norms which limited arbitrariness, and ensured t business was strictly supervized. But decisions only emerged wly, trivialities absorbed an inordinate amount of time, and ponsibility could never be clearly pinned to an individual. The eau system secured individual responsibility, and hence deciness, unity and energy. It was able to draft documents speedily, l saved on personnel expenses. But it did have the danger of ivering administration up to the idiosyncracies of the individual cial.

Now it became a matter of considerable argument whether bureau system and bureaucracy were to be identified with e other. As we have seen the idea of bureaucracy as rule by offic was already current in Germany. Since the new system of admi tration was widely recognized as increasing the power of offic the identification of it with bureaucracy was not a difficult ste take. This can be clearly illustrated from the great *Brockh* encyclopaedia of 1819:

> The modern form of public administration executes w the pen everything which previously would have been d by word of mouth. Hence many pens are set into moti In every branch of administration bureaux or offices h multiplied, and have been accorded so great a power o citizens that in many countries a veritable bureaucracy, r by offices, has developed. This bureaucracy becomes creasingly dangerous as the previous custom of conduct business through *collegia* falls into disuse. The director a bureau, in addition to their authority over its person have acquired an often inordinate amount of power o citizens at large.[53]

For opponents of the German state the identification of the bur system and bureaucracy made an extremely useful polemical poi Thus the socialist Karl Heinzen offered an apparently neutral a technical definition of bureaucracy as 'an administrative struct where a single official controls the administration, as opposed the collegial structure where several officials work under a he but with definite rights to participate in administration on a coll tive basis'.[54] But Heinzen then went on to make use of all negative connotations of bureaucracy as government by officials. its spirit it combined arrogance with servility; intended as an inst ment it acquired for itself the characteristics of unlimited pow Prussian officialdom was particularly sensitive to this kind of cri cism (Heinzen was forced to leave Germany) because it did necessarily have to come from socialist quarters. It was quite co sistent with this idea of bureaucracy to call on the monarch re-establish true statesmanship, as another critic of bureaucra Friedrich Rohmer, did when he argued that the only tangi result of the 1848 revolutions was to put new men into the administrative system.[55]

By and large the 'official' representatives (and it must be remem-
red that professors were employees of the state) of German
litical science tried to maintain the distinction between the new
stem of administration and bureaucracy. Sometimes this distinc-
n simply took the form of asserting that the term 'bureaucracy'
s used in two quite different ways, which were not to be confused
th each other.[56] Sometimes, as in the eleventh edition of *Brock-
us*, the term was reserved for the case where officials controlled
te affairs, and the new administrative structure was simply
signated *Bureausystem*.[57] Lorenz von Stein preferred the latter
ıge.[58]

This semantic confusion, coupled with the prevalence of pole-
cs against bureaucracy, prompted the first academic analysis of
: concept of bureaucracy in 1846.[59] Robert von Mohl, professor
political science at Heidelberg, suggested that historically the
aning of bureaucracy as the 'bureau system' had priority, and
d only recently been supplanted by the popular abusive mean-
g. But as a term of abuse von Mohl found that bureaucracy had
variety of connotations, depending on which social group was
ering the complaint. The privileged classes complained of loss
privileges, the commercial classes of interference in commerce,
isans of paperwork, scientists of ignorance, statesmen of delay.
hind all these expressions of complaint lay a common idea of
reaucracy as 'the false conception of the tasks of the state,
plemented by a numerous . . . body of professional officials'.[60]

Von Mohl was a standard authority to be quoted in nineteenth-
ıtury encyclopaedias. Hence it is important to note a shift of
phasis in his concept of bureaucracy. Earlier concepts were part
a system of concepts, however rudimentary. De Gournay
ought of bureaucracy as one of four types of government,
inzen as one of two types of administrative system. Von Mohl
ıply relied upon finding a common meaning in colloquial usage.
ıere citizens complained about the state, there, *ipso facto*, was
reaucracy. Such complaints could be assuaged by governmental
ntion to improving education, reducing form-filling and by
ıeral goodwill. Compared with a writer such as Mill, von Mohl
s simply considering contingent features of bureaucracy, super-
al symptoms rather than the underlying condition. (These were
quently referred to as bureaucratism.) Since any form of govern-
nt was likely to engender similar complaints it was an easy step

to regard any system of administration, good or bad, as bureaucra and this somewhat vapid usage, very popular in the twentie century, emerged soon after von Mohl's essay.[61]

Bureaucratism—the behaviour and attitudes of professio officials which offended the citizen—received its fullest discussi in the work of Josef Olszewski, a Polish lawyer, in 1904.[62] His lo account of administrative abuses owed much to von Mohl. T was also the theme of the first serious French account of burea cracy by the great social scientist, Frederic Le Play.[63] Inde more explicitly than any other writer, Le Play located bureaucra in the middle ranks of officialdom. For him it meant the dissem ation of authority among minor officials, absorbed in deta intent upon complicating business, and suppressing initiative others.

The popular success of Balzac's characterization of bureaucra had seemed to remove the topic from serious political analysis France.[64] The classic analysis of the French governmental syst by de Tocqueville made only passing reference to bureaucracy a concentrated on the processes of centralization.[65] This factor, gether with the absence of the bureaucratic-collegial dichotomy German administrative science accounted for the distinctiven of Le Play's approach. Sharply distinguishing bureaucracy fr centralization, he attempted to provide a structural and moti tional explanation of the behaviour of middle-ranking offici

Le Play's concern was with organizational structure rather th with legal concepts. This concern with the quality rather than legality of administration had something in common with Bageho concern for business efficiency. It clearly opened the way for co parisons between governmental and private methods of admin tration. When Pierre Leroy-Beaulieu, a liberal professor of politi wrote on the modern state and its functions in 1890 he took it granted that one could talk of bureaucracy in joint-stock co panies.[66] He found this form of bureaucracy far more supple a better staffed than the bureaucracy of the state. Such comparis were precursors of the twentieth-century concern with develop a general theory of organization.

The major nineteenth-century themes

It is possible to distinguish three major concepts in ni teenth-century writing on bureaucracy. Writers such as urnay or Mill saw bureaucracy as a major form of government, be compared and contrasted with monarchy, democracy or tocracy. German administrative theorists and polemicists, such Heinzen, concentrated on the particular form nineteenth-tury German administrative arrangements took. Von Mohl, zewski, or Le Play took their cue from popular discontent with ernment and saw the essence of bureaucracy in the officiousness he paid civil servant.

n spite of the twentieth-century neglect of this literature it is rly not insignificant, either in quantity or quality. The three or concepts distinguished here will have an important place in subsequent account of twentieth-century writing. Indeed it is y by referring to the substance of this chapter that it is possible make sense of later conceptual paradoxes. Two incompatible cepts—bureaucracy as administrative efficiency and bureau-cy as administrative inefficiency—compete for space in twenti-century theory. This is not an incomprehensible vagary of dern social science, but a development of nineteenth-century ument, mediated by the giant contributions of Mosca, Michels Max Weber.

ut if it is the case that the nineteenth-century writing is import-, both in its own right and for the understanding of later develop-nts, we are forced to ask why it has been lost to view. Mosca, chels and Max Weber appear both to have transformed the ory of bureaucracy and to have concealed its origins. A brief tentative answer to this puzzle may be offered if we consider v writing on bureaucracy differed from the work of the major itical ideologists of the nineteenth century.

With the exception of Mill, none of the writers considered nerto comes into the category of influential system builders. In great ideological systems one may distinguish two major ories of the distribution of power in society. In the one, those o held power were justified in either religious or secular meta-ysical terms. They had a mission to perform for God or society their servants, the public officials, shared in that purpose. In other, power was the product of a group's place in the economic er of society. Officials were simply the agents of government, instruments of the dominant class. We can see these two essen-ly simple standpoints elaborated by Hegel and Marx respec-ely. For neither did bureaucracy pose a problem of analysis since it could not be conceived of as a separate element disti from the state or the economic order. (Marx's position will examined in detail in chapter 4.)

But for lesser figures, more concerned to confront the syst with the facts, bureaucracy posed a severe analytical probl Each of the three major concepts of bureaucracy that have b distinguished here is focused on the paradoxical position of permanent, paid government official. For those who had faith a monarch or a sovereign people the official appeared more more distinct from the source of his authority, often in opposi to it, and certainly devoid of any charisma. For those who government as simply an aspect of the activity of men pursu their economic interests, the position of the official was paradoxi his involvement in power did not stem from his position in soci on the contrary, his position in society was derived from his p in government.

The facts were noted. But they were not accommodated in major theoretical system. Indeed when writers on bureaucr considered, as they all did, how it might be combated, their res was to the traditional formulas. Sometimes they called upon monarch to re-establish his authority. More frequently the rem was sought in the devolution of power into the hands of traditio interest groups: aristocracies, landowners, businessmen or t paying citizens. What was not accepted was that the power of permanent paid official was an inevitable feature of mod government. Therefore the great systems were not refurbished find a place for bureaucracy. It was only with Mosca, Michels Max Weber that the systematic conceptualizations of the imp ance of the permanent paid official became more adequate to place he already held in society.

2/The Classical Formulations

Mosca and Michels

In some rather obvious ways Gaetano Mosca's work belongs he nineteenth century. His classic work, *Elementi di Scienza tica* (translated as *The Ruling Class*) appeared in 1895.[1] His ting point was a criticism of the traditional classification of rnments. Broad comparative scope and the widest possible of historical evidence were characteristic of the works of Comte Spencer, the two writers Mosca found it most important to yse. Moreover, he was well aware of the nineteenth-century ition of writing on bureaucracy. Mill and Fischel were two of writers he listed as having most influence upon his own ries.[2]

he ingredients of Mosca's work were not new. But his com- tion of them was novel, and provides the justification for dis- ing him outside the nineteenth-century context. At last the cept of bureaucracy and dissatisfaction with the traditional me of governmental types were incorporated into a major parative analysis of politics. Against a classification of govern- ts which had endured for over two thousand years Mosca ly felt it was not too much to pit the major part of his fifty s of intellectual product. In 1884, in the first chapter of his book, he wrote: 'Now when we come to the classification of rnments which goes back to Aristotle and is still in our day ersally accepted: into democratic, aristocratic, or monarchic s . . . then we should expect that classification also to be based e most important, the essential characteristics of government not on mere trivialities and appearances.'[3] In 1933, in the last ter of his last book, he argued that this classification had two ts. It was 'based on observation of a single moment in the tion of political organisms', and it took into account their al rather than the really substantial differences'.[4]

the terminology of traditional logic Mosca was seeking a new *mentum divisionis*, a principle of classification, which would

get behind the language of authority and illuminate the realit
political processes.[5] He saw the core of this reality in the fact
power. In the following general proposition he summed up t
facts: 'In all regularly constituted societies in which somet
called a government exists, . . . the ruling class, or rather, t
who hold the exercise of the public power, will always be
minority and below them we find a numerous class of persons
never do, in any real sense, participate in government but me
submit to it: and these may be called the ruled class.'[6] '
observation formed the basis of Mosca's new classificatio
governments.

In *The Ruling Class* he divided all governments into two ty
the feudal and the bureaucratic.[7] In the feudal state the ru
class was simple in structure. Any member of it could exe
economic, judicial, administrative or military functions, and
could exercise direct and personal authority over a member o
ruled class. But in the bureaucratic state these functions
sharply separated from each other and became the exclusive ac
ties of particular sections of the ruling class. Among these sect
was a group whose presence gave the bureaucratic state its n
A portion of national wealth was allocated to a body of sala
officials, a bureaucracy.

There were two things in Mosca's analysis well calculate
shock nineteenth-century opinion. His emphasis on the ir
tability of minority rule apparently rendered any theor
democracy irrelevant. Secondly, public officials, instead of b
regarded as a useful adjunct to a duly constituted sovereign autho
were seen not only as a part of the ruling class in the modern
but as its defining characteristic.[8] For these reasons he has c
been regarded as a precursor of Italian fascism. But when we
to the less read parts of his theory, where he elaborated the
of the bureaucracy in the ruling class, we find that this wa
from his intentions.[9]

Mosca was very far from believing that the ruling class ha
be monolithic. He rejected the Marxian notion of an identit
interests among those in a similar class position. Instead he
the very possibility of liberty depend upon the differentiatio
the ruling class. Where a bureaucracy monopolized wealth
military power he spoke of bureaucratic absolutism. This for
government was 'despotism in its worst form': 'we get a

verful oligarchy, a more all-embracing "racket", than has ever n seen'.[10] It was essential that a bureaucracy be limited by resentative bodies. Through the mechanism of the vote the lers of different social forces could 'have themselves elected' to h bodies.[11] In this way the ruling class would be a reflection of varied interests and talents of a society.

Of course, consistent with his programme of analysing politics in istic terms, Mosca could not afford to be any more sanguine ut the operations of parliaments than he was about majority . He readily admitted that elected assemblies might not be able xercise sufficient control upon bureaucracy. Hence, as a further ck, he drew upon what he considered to be the lesson of glish experience. He called for direct involvement in adminis- ion by honorary public servants drawn from both the wealthy from 'respectable, hard-working people who live in moderate s'.[12]

Clearly Mosca's innovatory zeal was confined to scientific analy- The political system he advocated differed little from the blue- nts of Mill or Fischel. His importance is not that he differed n nineteenth-century liberals on the need to check bureaucracy that, agreeing with them on this, he reached the same clusions on the basis of a different analysis.

None the less it is also true that Mosca's dispassionate method an example which, followed by others, could easily produce ults far more destructive to ideas of representative government n his were. In particular his idea of bureaucracy was suscep- e to much more elaboration. He did not feel the need to define eaucracy, possibly because it does not appear to have meant to anything more complex than a body of public officials. What- r had some connection with such a body he called 'bureau- tic'.[13] When he wrote of the 'bureaucratic state' he mentioned racteristics of specialization and centralization which belonged t, but the essential feature was clearly the use of salaried em- yees in public services.[14] This apparent crudity was a conse- nce of what Mosca set out to achieve. He wished to bring cussions of bureaucracy and democracy into the realm of science neutralizing the terminology, and, to realize this, Mosca aimed macroscopic categorization of governments after the fashion of schemes of Comte and Spencer, which commanded high pres- as examples of social science. In other words Mosca put the

concept of bureaucracy into a new context. He brought it from
arena of political argument and offered it as a major category to
still embryonic science of sociology. But he went no further. T
first to do so was Robert Michels.

Concerned as he was to examine the implications of his dic
tomous classification of governments, Mosca only hinted at
reasons for a bureaucracy's position in the ruling class of a mod
state. Michels's *Political Parties* (1911), took up this theme.[15]
agreed with Mosca that a bureaucracy was a necessity in the m
ern state. In this way the politically dominant classes maintai
their position, while the insecure middle classes sought security
state employment. But there was no need to confine analysis to
state if one wished to discover the reasons for the rise of bure
cracies. Implicitly Mosca regarded the state as *sui generis*. Ho
ever, if one viewed it as an instance of a more embracing categ
the organization, and investigated the general features of mod
organizational structure, a more fundamental series of reas
could be revealed.

'Who says organization, say oligarchy,' was Michels's aphori
expression of those fundamental reasons.[16] Drawing his data fr
the history of political parties, he showed how the leaders of bo
with thousands of members found it necessary to recruit full-ti
salaried officials. These employees became specialists in vari
aspects of the organization's requirements. The leaders in th
turn required skills and education appropriate for managin
hierarchy of officials. They became a professional leadership, cut
from the general membership by a different cultural backgrou
Naturally the hierarchy of officials depended upon party reven
for their salaries. They therefore avoided any steps which mi
endanger the size of the membership. Thus, from a mea
organization becomes an end.[17]

Salaried officials were not peculiar to the state. Any large orga
zation required them in the modern world. However, Michels
only extended Mosca's thesis to all organizations: he stated it i
more deterministic form. He too reviewed the possibilities
limiting bureaucracy. He considered referenda, syndicalism, a
anarchism, but concluded that nothing could withstand 'the i
law of oligarchy'. Perhaps the most that could be expected
that a general consciousness of the oligarchical processes co
help to mitigate their rigours.[18]

The determinism of Michels's approach may well have contri-
ted to his showing little more interest in the concept of bureau-
cy than Mosca had done. If the salaried official was an inevitable
ture of the modern organization, and oligarchy the necessary
ult, there was little point to analysing the varied forms it might
e. The end-product was the same. The simplicity of Mosca's
l Michels's concept of bureaucracy—a body of salaried officials
may be seen as the counterpart of their dramatic dismissal of the
nplex structure of democratic constitutional thought. It facili-
ed a sociological analysis of the realities of power on a broad
l general level. But it was far from the detailed characterization
their contemporary Olszewski,[19] and was only loosely linked
h the concepts of power, administration and authority which
re an essential part of the analysis. It was Max Weber who took
the huge task of advancing the sociological account of Mosca
l Michels, and at the same time doing justice to the high degree
refinement that the concept of bureaucracy had reached in
n-sociological literature.

Max Weber: the theory of organization

In terms of the influence it has exerted and the argument it
stimulated Weber's writing on bureaucracy is more important
n the sum total of the contributions which have already been
cussed. Yet there is a dearth of detailed exposition of his work,
opposed to straightforward borrowing of particular ideas on the
e hand, or critical discussions of some fragment of his writing
the other.[20] This is not surprising in view of the variety of ver-
ns that he left. Two important sources appeared in his post-
mous *Wirtschaft und Gesellschaft* (1921).[21] Apart from them,
erences to bureaucracy are scattered throughout the two mas-
e volumes of that work. A third vital source, his lengthy essay
arliament and Government in the Newly-Organized Germany"
18), has only recently been translated into English and has been
duly neglected.[22]

The results of these difficulties with Weber's text have been
adoxical. He placed more emphasis than any other of the
nding fathers of modern sociology upon clarity and coherence
concept-formation. What he wrote about bureaucracy is part of
rodigious effort to codify the concepts of social science. The
perficial lucidity of Mosca's and Michels's theses avoided asking

vital conceptual questions, such as, 'What do we mean by pow or by administration, authority, the official?' and the many c cepts which a discussion of bureaucracy involves. Yet the dee coherence of Weber's approach, which sprang from asking a offering answers to such questions, has been overshadowed by dramatic unity of their themes. By contrast, Weber's treatment bureaucracy has often been considered as a set of isolated *aperç* At best it has been seen as the expression of either his gene methodology or a philosophy of history.[23]

The remainder of this chapter will offer an exposition of Webe theory of bureaucracy which emphasizes that it is grounded i large set of related concepts. In order to let the lines of his ar ment stand out as clearly as possible the arguments of his m critics will be reserved until the next chapter.

The most relevant conceptual context for such an expositio to be found in Weber's analysis of organization. In the first chap of *Wirtschaft und Gesellschaft*, where he examined the basic c cepts of sociology, Weber devoted considerable attention to idea of a *Verband*.[24] This was clearly a concept of very wide sig ficance since it comprised such differing notions as the state, political party, the church, the sect and the firm. 'Organization perhaps the most obvious translation, but in any case *Verband* h a special connotation for Weber.[25] It signified an ordering of so relationships, the maintenance of which certain individuals too their special task. The presence of a leader and usually also an ministrative staff was the defining characteristic of an organizati It was they who preserved the structure. In this remarkably su mary manner, Weber incorporated the major point of Mosca's a Michels's analyses. By definition organizations were hierarc bi- or tri-partite structures.

Weber regarded the fact that human behaviour was regula oriented to a set of rules (*Ordnung*) as basic to sociological analy The existence of a distinctive set of rules governing behaviour intrinsic to the concept of an organization. Without them it wo not be possible to say what was and what was not organizatio behaviour. The rules of an organization Weber termed the admi trative order (*Verwaltungsordung*).[26] The administrative staff (*V waltungsstab*) had a dual relationship to these rules. On the one ha its own behaviour was regulated by them. On the other it had task of seeing that the rest of the membership adhered to then

The most important aspect of the administrative order was that determined who was to give commands to whom. Administra-n and authority (*Herrschaft*) were intimately linked. 'Every form authority expresses itself and functions as administration. Every m of administration in some way requires authority, since its ection demands that some sort of power to command is vested someone.'[28] This is one of the most striking instances of the portance Weber attached to what has also been called imperative ordination.[29] Commands and rules ranked as equally important tors in the structuring of social relationships. In an administra-e order they were linked in that the rules regulated the scope d possession of authority.

In the Weberian organization with an administrative staff each mber was in the position of either giving or receiving orders. e staff both gave and received. It was in this context of examin-; the basic categories of organizational structure that Weber veloped his famous distinction between power (*Macht*) and hority. A person could be said to have power if 'within a social ationship, his own will could be enforced despite resistance'.[30] t such a broad concept, Weber commented, was 'sociologically orphous'.[31] Individuals could be said to have power in all kinds ways. For the structuring of human groups it was 'a special tance of power' which was most important.[32] This 'special tance' was authority. It existed when 'a command of a finite content found obedience on the part of specific indi-duals'.[33]

It cannot be regarded as fortuitous that Weber developed the nceptual distinction between power and authority in the course his discussion of organizational structure. He made explicit erence to the theory of minority power in organizations in an ly essay on authority.[34] But while drawing attention to the fac-s which favoured oligarchy he stressed that obedience to com-nds was primarily dependent upon a belief in their legitimacy, elief that the orders were justified and that it was right to obey. other words Weber was arguing that it was important not to mp from the facts of orders being given and accepted to the con-sion that those giving the orders had other kinds of power. terpreted as a gloss on Mosca, Weber was cautioning against tomatically regarding every civil servant as a member of the ling class.

It was the idea of legitimacy which provided Weber with principle for classifying organizations. In his strongest stateme on the subject he said: 'The foundation of all authority, and hen of all compliance with orders, is a belief in prestige, which opera to the advantage of the ruler or rulers.'[35] With different forms belief in the legitimacy of authority were associated differe authority structures and hence organizational forms.

Weber identified three kinds of such beliefs. The first was t obedience was justified because the person giving the order h some sacred or altogether outstanding characteristic. This Web termed 'charismatic authority'. Secondly, a command might obeyed out of reverence for old-established patterns of order 'traditional authority'. Thirdly, men might believe that a pers giving an order was acting in accordance with his duties as stip lated in a code of legal rules and regulations. This was Webe category of 'legal authority', which, he added, was of a ratior character. It was the type of authority which characterized t modern organization, and with it was associated increasingly bureaucratic administrative staff.[36]

It was at this point, therefore, among the categories of organiz tional analysis that the concept of bureaucracy became relevant. was introduced into an already sharply defined conceptual fie (This was, of course, in turn part of an even more general schen of concepts for the analysis of social action. It also included mo specialized distinctions which would take too long to introduce this context.)

In a schematic overview of that conceptual field we may di tinguish three groups of concepts. First there were the concep which distinguished between different statuses in the organizatio i.e. the leadership, the administrative staff and the general men bership. Secondly, there were the concepts which helped to speci the relationship between those statuses, i.e. the administrati order, authority and legitimacy. Finally, the ideas of charism tradition and legality were introduced as a means of classifyi different authority structures. We must now see how Weber's id of bureaucracy fitted into this scheme.

Max Weber: the concept of bureaucracy

Weber never defined bureaucracy. This is surprising in tw ways. It is regularly assumed that he did make such a definitic d his failure to do so is in marked contrast to his efforts to define e other concepts of organizational analysis. Indeed it is clear that eber did not regard the term 'bureaucracy' as part of the language social science. It is notable how frequently he enclosed it in otation marks to indicate that it had been lifted from everyday rlance.[37] What he did take care to do was to specify the features what he considered the most rational form of bureaucracy. But s general concept of bureaucracy, as opposed to this specific pe, must be constructed by inference from the large number of ssages where he made allusion to it.

One clue to Weber's general concept is provided by his identi-ation of another kind of bureaucracy apart from the most rational pe. This was patrimonial bureaucracy.[38] It differed from the tional type primarily because it depended upon unfree officials ther than contractually appointed men. Weber found examples this in the later Roman Empire, in ancient Egypt, and in the yzantine Empire. But clearly intrinsic to the notion of patri-onial bureaucracy was the existence of a body of officials. The ncept of an official (*Beamter*) was basic to that of bureaucracy. his is borne out by the frequent occasions on which Weber used *eamtentum* (officialdom) as an alternative to bureaucracy.[39]

Weber wrote a great deal about the place of the official in modern ciety. It was for him an increasingly important type of social le. The distinctive features of this role were, first of all, that the dividual had specified duties to perform and, secondly, that the cilities and resources necessary for fulfilling those duties were ovided by someone other than the role holder. In these respects e official was in the same position as the factory worker, and Veber explicitly referred to Marx's theory of the modern separa-on of the individual from the means of production.[40] But the ficial had a characteristic which distinguished him from the orker: he had authority.

Since the official had authority, and, at the same time, this was nferred upon him, it goes almost without saying that an official as involved in administration ('every form of authority expresses self and functions as administration', see above p. 39). To speak f administrative officials would, for Weber, be pleonastic. But this eant that the concept of an official was bound to comprise many ore occupational categories than might at first appear to be the ase. The modern army officer, the Roman Catholic bishop, the factory manager were all officials also, spending much of their ti in their offices interpreting and transmitting written instruction

However, Weber did not include all officials within the noti of a bureaucracy. The elected official or the one selected by lot explicitly refused to call bureaucratic. The essential feature of t bureaucratic official was that he was an appointee.[41] In making tl point Weber came his nearest to making a definition of his gene usage of bureaucracy. 'No exercise of authority can be purely bu eaucratic', he wrote, 'i.e. purely through contractually engaged a appointed officials.'[42]

Perhaps both the technical background and the generality Weber's concept of bureaucracy can be conveyed in a definition this kind: by bureaucracy is meant an administrative body appointed officials. It is noteworthy how close such a formulati is to the concepts of Michels and Mosca. Like them Weber thoug of bureaucracy as a collective term for a body of officials, a defin and distinct group whose work and influence could be seen in kinds of organizations. But it is also true that Weber stressed ce tain organizational features, in particular appointment procedur which meant that even in his general concept of bureaucracy we comprised not only the idea of a group but also the notion of di tinct forms of action. This became even more important in Webe concept of the most rational type of bureaucracy.

In spite of the fact that up to this point it has been stressed th Weber had a general concept of bureaucracy, it is none the le true that this was overshadowed in importance, both for him ar subsequent commentators, by its so-called rational variant. Inde to some extent Weber was inconsistent. Sometimes he spoke bureaucracy in a general and broad sense, at other times he r served the term for his pure and rational type. A full explanati of this would demand an exploration of Weber's theories of soci scientific concept-formation.[43] It may suffice to say that, wh faced with a widely disseminated concept of vague outline b broad historical significance, Weber preferred to offer a preci and detailed characterization of the phenomenon as it might appe over a very brief period of time (or, in its complete details, neve rather than to attempt a definition which, in its comprehe siveness, would lack specificity and clarity. This did not, as w have seen, prevent him from writing about bureaucracy in general sense, especially in polemical contexts.

Weber considered rational bureaucracy as a major element in the tionalization of the modern world, for him the most important of social processes. Among other things this process involved owing precision and explicitness in the principles governing cial organization. This in itself facilitated and encouraged social ientific conceptualization, and the conceptual underpinning of eber's theory of bureaucracy is at its clearest when he discussed e rational pure type.

In conformity with his theory that a belief in legitimacy was sic to nearly all systems of authority he began by setting out five lated beliefs on which legal authority depended.[44] In abbreviated rm these were:

I That a legal code can be established which can claim obedience from members of the organization.

II That the law is a system of abstract rules which are applied to particular cases, and that administration looks after the interests of the organization within the limits of that law.

III That the man exercising authority also obeys this impersonal order.

IV That only *qua* member does the member obey the law.

V That obedience is due not to the person who holds authority but to the impersonal order which has granted him this position.

On the basis of these conceptions of legitimacy Weber was ole to formulate eight propositions about the structuring of legal thority sytems:

(*a*) Official tasks are organized on a continuous, regulated basis.

(*b*) These tasks are divided into functionally distinct spheres, each furnished with the requisite authority and sanctions.

(*c*) Offices are arranged hierarchically, the rights of control and complaint between them being specified.

(*d*) The rules according to which work is conducted may be either technical or legal. In both cases trained men are necessary.

(*e*) The resources of the organization are quite distin from those of the members as private individuals.

(*f*) The office holder cannot appropriate his office.

(*g*) Administration is based on written documents and t tends to make the office (*Bureau*) the hub of t modern organization.

(*h*) Legal authority systems can take many forms, but a seen at their purest in a bureaucratic administrati staff.[45]

The last proposition is vital for the understanding of Weber thinking on bureaucracy. The five conceptions of legitimacy a the eight principles of authority were exhibited in the organizatio of the bureaucratic administrative staff, but they did not in then selves warrant talking of bureaucracy. Other kinds of administr tion, e.g. collegial or honorary, could also be based on the propositions and Weber discussed them at length (see ne section). Weber also added that it was possible to have a bureau cratic administrative staff when the leadership did not base itse on the legal rational principles.

The bureaucractic administrative staff, the bureaucracy in i most rational form, presupposed the preceding propositions c legitimacy and authority, and had the following defining chara teristics:

1 The staff members are personally free, observing onl the impersonal duties of their offices.

2 There is a clear hierarchy of offices.

3 The functions of the offices are clearly specified.

4 Officials are appointed on the basis of a contract.

5 They are selected on the basis of a professional qual fication, ideally substantiated by a diploma gaine through examination.

6 They have a money salary, and usually pension right The salary is graded according to position in the hier archy. The official can always leave the post, and unde certain circumstances it may also be terminated.

7 The official's post is his sole or major occupation.

8 There is a career structure, and promotion is possible either by seniority or merit, and according to the judgement of superiors.

9 The official may appropriate neither the post nor the resources which go with it.

10 He is subject to a unified control and disciplinary system.[46]

These ten features constituted Max Weber's renowned eal, pure or most rational type of bureaucracy: the kind of ministrative staff which he frequently referred to *tout court* as ureaucracy'. Without a doubt the single most important state- ent on the subject in the social sciences, its influence has been mense. Not only has it blotted out the literature which was dis- ssed in the previous chapter, to a major extent it has dominated own context in Weber's writing. In the previous section its con- ptual foundation was examined. In the next a further specifica- n of the context, where Weber attempted to bind his theory of ganization to the theory of democracy will be considered.

Max Weber: the limits on bureaucracy

Weber was sure that rational bureaucracy was bound to crease in importance. It had a series of characteristics—precision, ntinuity, discipline, strictness, reliability—which made it tech- cally the most satisfactory form of organization, both for author- y holders and all other interested parties: 'The development of odern organizational forms in all spheres (state, church, army, arty, the economy, interest groups, voluntary associations, chari- ble bodies or whatever) is simply identical with the development nd continuous increase of bureaucratic administration.'[47] On everal occasions Weber expressed the view that bureaucratization as an inevitable process.[48] By bureaucratization Weber meant the rowth of the ten features he listed as aspects of rational bureau- racy. But as part of the general process of rationalization it tended imply also the separation of men from the means of production nd the general growth of formalism in organizations.[49]

Weber viewed this process with pessimistic resignation but at no oint did he coin a term for, nor indeed pay much attention to, the henomena of red tape and bureaucratic inefficiency which had so reoccupied Olszewski and his predecessors. 'Bureaucratism', which had often been used to designate bureaucratic abuses, Web used once or twice but without signifying anything more than t special nature of bureaucratic activity.[50] He did not need such term very frequently since, by defining his bureaucratic admini trative staff in terms of organization and duties, when he spoke bureaucracy the activities of the bureaucrat were implied. But t fact that Weber neglected to examine the inefficiencies of mode administration became, as we shall see in the next chapter, a maj debating issue.

However, if Weber minimized the theme of inefficiency, he ma up for this by paying close attention to the problem of bureaucrat power. For with bureaucratization went the growth of the power the officials. It is of great importance to note that this was not matter of the definition of bureaucratization. That the bureaucr acquired power was an empirical statement. The sources of th power could be seen in the special knowledge which the offici possessed. In the first place he had a specialist's knowledge of di ciplines essential to administration in the modern world, e.g. ec nomics or law. Secondly, in the course of his duties he acquired great deal of concrete information, much of it artificially restricte by ideas of confidentiality and secrecy.

Convinced as he was that bureaucratization was inevitable, an that bureaucrats gained power, none the less Weber resisted an identification of bureaucracy with rule by officials. Indeed it woul scarcely be an exaggeration to say that by taking the distinctio between power and authority up to the point of insisting that elec ted officials were not bureaucratic Weber was intent on ensurin that bureaucracy could be analysed without prejudging the issu of the possibility of democracy. De Gournay, Mill and Michel three very different writers, all represented a school of though which saw bureaucracy and democracy as opposite and mutuall exclusive systems of government. In contrast, Weber's analysi was designed to show that the specific nature of modern adminis tration and the control of the apparatus of the modern state wer conceptually distinct.

In spite of the far more highly developed system of concepts, i would be a mistake to infer that Weber was uninterested in th traditional problem of the relation between democracy and bureau cracy. His analytical refinement was not designed to leave thi problem behind. On the contrary, his concern for it was the mos ıportant motivation behind his interest in bureaucracy. His ngest and most important essay in political polemics, "Parliment and Government in the Newly Organized Germany" (1918), as centred upon the problem of *Beamtenherrschaft* in the German ate. *Beamtenherrschaft*—rule by officials—was a concept which 'eber kept quite distinct from bureaucracy. It was a danger which :ose out of bureaucracy and Weber considered it to be realized in ıe direst form in Germany under Bismarck. He held that Bismarck ad enfeebled Germany by allowing officials to occupy decisive ositions in the state. The result was a politically stultified nation, ith the vigour of the non-bureaucratic classes unable to express self.

The problem Weber considered was how the inherent tendency f bureaucracy to accumulate power could be prevented from eaching the point where it controlled the policy and action of the rganization it was supposed to serve. In this neglected area of his vork Weber considered a very large number of mechanisms for miting the scope of systems of authority generally and bureaucracy in particular.[51] These mechanisms fell into five major ategories.

1 *Collegiality*. The attention Weber paid to this concept provides useful evidence of the extent to which his idea of bureaucracy was influenced by nineteenth-century German administrative heory. Bureaucracy, for him, meant that, at each stage of the official hierarchy, one person, and one person only, had the responibility for taking a decision. As soon as others were involved in that lecision, *as of right*, then the collegial principle was being employed. Weber distinguished twelve forms of collegiality. Among hem were included such arrangements as the Roman consulate, he British cabinet, various kinds of senates and parliaments. Weber considered that collegiality would always have an important part to play in limiting bureaucracy, but that its disadvantages in erms of speed of decision and attribution of responsibility meant hat it had everywhere receded in the face of the monocratic principle.

2 *The Separation of Powers*. Bureaucracy involved the division of tasks into relatively distinct functional spheres. Separation of powers meant dividing responsibility for the same function

between two or more bodies. For any decision to emerge a co promise between them had to be reached. Weber mentioned t compromise over the budget which historically had to be reach by the British monarch and Parliament. Weber regarded such system as inherently unstable. One of the authorities was bound win pre-eminence.

3 *Amateur Administration.* When a government did n pay its administrators it was dependent upon those who had t resources to permit their spending time in unremunerated activi Such men also had to have sufficient public esteem to comma general confidence. This system could not measure up to the d mands for expertise which modern society made, and whe amateurs were assisted by professionals it was always the lat who made the real decisions.

4 *Direct Democracy.* There were several devices for ensu ing that officials were guided directly by, and answerable to, a assembly. Short term of office, selection by lot, permanent poss bility of recall were all designed to serve this end. Only in the sma organization, as in some forms of local government, was this feasible method of administration. Here too the need for experti was a decisive counterweight.

5 *Representation.* The claim of a leader to represent h followers was nothing new. Both charismatic and traditional leade made such claims. But what was novel in the modern world w the existence of collegial representative bodies, whose membe were selected by vote and were free to make decisions and share i authority over those who had elected them. Such a system coul not be understood except in relation to the operation of politic parties, themselves bureaucratized, but it was through th medium that Weber saw the greatest possibility of a check o bureaucracy.

Weber considered the free parliament in the modern sta to be of vital importance in giving expression to the differen interest groups which the capitalist economy engendered. Throug the party system such groups could find leaders for these assem blies. And in the parliamentary struggle men of real quality, fitte to lead a world power, could be discovered. The Germans did no lize, Weber argued, that the English Parliament acted as a prov- ground for political leaders. In important respects Weber's thusiasm for the representative system owed more to his con- tion that national greatness depended on finding able leaders in to any concern for democratic values.[52]

This point is substantiated by the fact that Weber did not regard reaucratization of political parties as a fundamental obstacle to presentative government. On the contrary, the complexity of odern party administration meant that the party leader had ac- ired essential knowledge of the techniques of modern adminis- tion before entering high office. The party leader was not a lettante. He could exercise real control over state administration. rthermore the modern party machine demanded discipline and utine. In this way it helped to combat the dangers of demagoguery.

Just as with Mosca, Weber's analysis of bureaucracy led to a ea for adherence to representative government, and for reasons nilar to Mosca's. It was not ideally democratic. But it did the ost that could be expected under the conditions of modern tionalized society. It steered a middle course between the Scylla mass irrationality and the Charybdis of bureaucratic tyranny.

3/The Debate with Weber

The sources of Weber's theory

It is not possible to deny the huge advance in sophisticati which distinguished Max Weber's theory of bureaucracy from i nineteenth-century predecessors. As we saw in the first chapte there were several distinct strands in nineteenth-century thinki on bureaucracy. It was Weber's achievement to bring them t gether. To assess his work in this way appears to cast doubt upo its novelty. But, paradoxically, there was a major element novelty in Weber's theory which sprang from his neglect of o important aspect of earlier thought. Weber's lack of concern f the problem of bureaucratic inefficiency was in striking contrast much earlier writing, and has aroused a controversy which go on today. This chapter will consider that controversy, and wi incidentally, provide an introduction to many of the most importa themes in the modern study of bureaucracy.

Before considering his critics' case, it is important to understan the intellectual pedigree of Weber's conceptualizations. It will pr vide some prior explanation of the imputed defects in his theo and will prepare the ground for the restatement of his position wit which this chapter concludes. Unfortunately it is not easy to mak precise attributions of influence where Weber's later work is co cerned. He rarely bothered with scholarly apparatus and we mu rely on indirect internal evidence. However we may detect fo major influences. These were German administrative theor Michels; Marx; and the doyen of German economic and soci historians, Gustav Schmoller.

Weber had trained as a lawyer and he wrote a monumental soc ology of law. His close acquaintance with German administrativ theory, which was a part of a normal legal curriculum, can be take for granted. It is therefore not surprising that a great deal of h characterization of the ideal type echoed that theory. In particula the clear contrast he drew between monocratic and collegial ad ministration and his balance sheet of their relative advantages an

advantages could have been found in any administrative text-
ok from the early nineteenth century onwards (see above, p. 29).
rtainly he found there every precedent for viewing state adminis-
tion as the epitome of efficiency. But it will be recalled that those
orists resisted the application of the label 'bureaucracy' to their
odels of perfect administration. That he was able to do so without
ise of paradox owed something at least to Michels.

Weber's interest in bureaucracy certainly pre-dated the publi-
ion of Michels's *Political Parties*. Indeed in 1909, at a confer-
ce in Vienna, he caused a considerable storm by the vehemence
his views on the inappropriate extent of the bureaucrats' influ-
ce in German society.[1] But he knew Michels well, and they
ended the same conferences and informal gatherings. In
ichels's work he had a clear link, through Mosca, to the ninteenth-
ntury setting of the problem of the relation between bureaucracy
d democracy, and, at the same time, an example of the attempt
treat the issue in a neutral and scientific way. Michels did not
nt to enter into a harangue against the abuses of officialdom, but
the same time he wished to show the incompatibility of bureau-
acy and democracy. It suited him well to adopt as neutral as
ssible a concept of bureaucracy as a status group of administra-
e officials, and then to demonstrate ineluctable consequences in
e form of concentration of power. It was a way of thinking which
osca dubbed 'a-democratic' rather than 'anti-democratic'.[2]

Committed as he was to an objective social science, Weber
eded the term 'bureaucracy' to serve the same function in his
ork as it did for Michels. He did not wish to declaim against
reaucracy. Indeed it could be argued that he went in the oppo-
e direction when he stressed its rationality. It was the very
tionality of modern administration which raised problems for
mocracy. The concept of rational bureaucracy (a solecism in
rms of nineteenth-century thinking) summed up this issue in the
ortest possible way.

In spite of his affinity with Michels, it is hard not to see a note
criticism of that writer in Weber's first essay on bureaucracy.
ritten in the two years following *Political Parties*, this essay paid
pecially close attention to the problem of the power position of
e bureaucracy. He agreed that bureaucratization was universal in
e modern state but argued: 'The fact that bureaucratic organisa-
on is technically the most highly developed means of power in the

hands of the man who controls it does not determine the weig that bureaucracy as such is capable of having in a particular soc structure.'[3] He likened the argument that the indispensability the bureaucrat gave him power to the belief that the indispens bility of the proletariat necessarily meant it would gain control the state. 'Whether the power of bureaucracy as such increases ca not be decided *a priori* from such reasons.'[4] As we have alrea seen, it was just this point which lay at the back of Weber's conce to distinguish power and authority.

A third influence which is clearly visible in Weber's concept bureaucracy is that of Marx. Weber likened the position of t official, giving orders he did not originate from a room which w not his own, to the position of Marx's expropriated worker, ow ing nothing but his labour power. It was not what Marx wro explicitly on bureaucracy which influenced Weber (it was s largely unpublished) but the general thesis on man's alienati which Weber transcended in his theory of rationalization. But respect of Weber's theory of the development of bureaucracy fro its patrimonial to rational forms his debt to Marx should not over-emphasized. For there was already in existence a develo mental account of the growth of administration which was a r markably precise anticipation of what Weber was to say. This w by Gustav Schmoller.

Schmoller, who had perhaps more prestige as a social and econ mic scientist than any other of his contemporaries in German was invited to edit and introduce a series of documents on t history of the Prussian administrative system, the *Acta Borussic* Schmoller wrote a general introduction to this in 1894, and in t same year gave a lecture on German officialdom.[5] These tw sources contain a brilliant interpretation of the rise of mode public administration.

Giving credit to Herbert Spencer as his inspiration, Schmoll began from the assumption that every society was constituted three parts: a leader, his staff and the masses. (As was shown in t previous chapter, Weber's analysis of organization was very sim lar.) Social development depended on the growing differentiati of these three component parts, while constitutional differenc between states stemmed from variations in their relative importanc

As far as the leader's staff was concerned, Schmoller found possible to distinguish four stages in its development. In the firs primitive communities, he discerned no genuine differentiation offices from other roles in society. There followed two stages ich overlapped in time. In the one, there were administrative ices filled hereditarily; in the other, offices were of short duration l filled by lot or election. The former characterized feudal soci-es, the latter was particularly prevalent in classical Greece and me. They both depended on a propertied, ruling aristocracy. In fourth and final stage of development they were replaced by a eer structure in which the official was a life-long professional. that it may be compared directly with Weber's formulation, it worth letting Schmoller speak for himself on this final stage. It olved:

> a life-long, salaried, professional job for the official, with a clear and fixed career structure for which specialized preparation is necessary. The official is normally appointed by the head of state, and his status, rights and duties are regulated in detail by a developed code of office law. This office structure is the product of an advancing division of labour. As in all earlier civilized nations, it is linked with the formation of social classes. It presupposes an already developed system of offices, which, however, the professional officials radically transform. It is assisted by higher education and the schools which have developed along side of the family. Above all it flourishes as a consequence of a money economy which permits remuneration in the form of salaries for specialized functions, in place of grants of land or support in the lord's household.[6]

Other aspects which Schmoller singled out included the rarchy of positions and salaries and the fact that it was on the sis of freely signed contracts that men gave their energies to the jectives of the administration. 'This system of offices has, from ne to time and in particular states, made great, indeed unsurssable, achievements, and even where it has not reached unalled authority, it has become an indispensable element in the of the modern state.'[7]

Of course, Schmoller conceded, such a development was not thout its darker side. Vom Stein's criticisms were not without ntent (see above, p. 19). Constant vigilance was necessary to ere the high quality of officials, and to prevent the dangers of bureaucracy. Quite in accord with the language of those who su ported the Prussian state, Schmoller saw bureaucracy as consisti of pathological deviations (of a remediable nature) from the norn course of sound administration.

There was little of a substantive nature for Weber to add Schmoller's account. His familiarity with it cannot be in dou Apart from filling in some of the technical legal detail his m contribution was to recast the conceptual framework. But this w sufficient to give a new direction to thinking about bureaucra By identifying bureaucracy with modern officialdom, Wet attempted both to neutralize that contentious concept and to sh that the problem of control was inherent in even the most perf administrative system. By describing such a system as rational made the ponderous formulations of German administrative theo an expression of a universal historical process.

Even for us, some fifty years after Weber wrote and duri which time his influence has been widely felt, some of the pa doxical and self-contradictory overtones of a concept of 'ratio bureaucracy' are still apparent. We can be sure they were for hi too. The concept summed up his deep ambivalence about t development of modern administration: his admiration for it as intellectual achievement; his conviction of its inexorable advan and his fear for its encroachments on individual and natior self-expression.

If it was calculated to create controversy, it certainly succeede Was the long tradition of writing on bureaucratic inefficiency besi the point? Was Weber's rational type of bureaucracy really rational as he made it out to be? Was the advance of rationaliz tion so certain? Such issues became the centre of one of the mo important themes in modern writing on bureaucracy.

The case against Weber

The simplest stricture of all which could be made agair Weber was that he created an unnecessary confusion in vocab lary. As one writer has put it: 'The disadvantages of the applicati of the words "bureaucracy" and "bureaucratic" to the norm structure of modern administration, as well as to its perversion, a an unncessary ambiguity and a partial, but incomplete, break wi everyday usage . . . his indiscriminate use of the term "burea cracy" was, therefore, particularly unfortunate.'[8] But, as we ha n, there were compelling reasons for Weber to use this term in te of (or, indeed, to some extent because of) the break with rmal usage. Whether his vocabulary was unfortunate depends the substantive issue of the cogency of his position. One form of ack on that position has been to question the rationality of eber's 'rational bureaucracy'.

One of the most well-known essays questioning the idea of ional bureaucracy is a short article by Robert Merton, "Bureau- tic Structure and Personality" (1940).[9] Merton argues that em- asis on precision and reliability in administration may well have f-defeating consequences. Rules, designed as means to ends, y well become ends in themselves. The graded career structure the bureaucrat may encourage him to an excess of the virtues he supposed to embody: prudence, discipline, method. Governed similar work conditions officials develop a group solidarity which y result in opposition to necessary change. Where officials are pposed to serve the public the very norms of impersonality which vern their behaviour may cause conflict with individual citizens. What Merton is stressing is that a structure which is rational in eber's sense can easily generate consequences which are unex- cted and detrimental to the attainment of an organization's jectives. In so doing he is reasserting, and providing a more phisticated vindication of, the pre-Weberian view that bureau- cy means inefficiency. (In this respect it is interesting to note t Merton cites Ramsay Muir as one of his sources.[10]) An analog- s version of what, in sociological language, Merton terms the sfunctional consequences of bureaucracy, is provided by the rk of Philip Selznick.[11] Concentrating upon the division of func- ns within an organization, he shows how sub-units set up goals their own which may conflict with the purposes of the organiza- n as a whole. The remedy for this, the setting up of new depart- nts to counteract the tendencies of the old, only exacerbates the uation by creating more sub-unit goals.

Neither Merton nor Selznick are concerned to point out incon- tencies in Weber's propositions on rational bureaucracy. Rather y intend to show that the formal specification of organizational ucture which he outlined is insufficient as a description of how reaucrats will in fact behave. The official has characteristics as a cial being beyond those which the administrative code specifies. ke other men he has interests, prejudices and fears. He forms friendships and cliques. In this respect both Merton and Selzn are applying to administration the major insights derived fr industrial sociology of the 1930s.[12] During that time substan empirical research was demonstrating the importance of infor group processes for morale and productivity in industry.

The internal consistency of Weber's ideal type has been calle question by one of the translators and editors of *Wirtschaft* *Gesellschaft*.[13] Talcott Parsons draws attention to the fact t Weber's administrative staff was defined as having professio expertise as well as the right to give orders. Such attributes, arg Parsons, may well give rise to conflict within bureaucracy, sinc will be impossible to ensure that high position in the hierarchy authority will be matched by equivalent professional skill. T problem for members of the organization will then arise of wh to obey, the person with the right to command or the man with greater expertise.

Parson's criticism is used as a starting point by Alvin Gould in his *Patterns of Industrial Bureaucracy* (1955), one of the m important and influential post-Weberian studies. Gouldner gene lizes the argument on the conflict of professional and bureaucra authority into an analysis of the bases of compliance within organization. He distinguishes two major types of bureaucra 'punishment-centred' and 'representative'. In the former, memb of the organization conform reluctantly to rules which they c sider to be imposed on them by an alien group. But, in the latt organizational members regard rules as necessary on techni grounds and in their own interests. The two different attitudes rules have a marked influence on the efficient working of organization.[14]

An argument similar to that of Gouldner is used by R. Francis and R. C. Stone in their *Service and Procedure in Burea cracy* (1956). They show that, although the official literature of organization may enjoin impersonality and a strict adherence fixed procedures, in practice the staff may adapt their action to s circumstances and the needs of individuals. Gouldner, Francis a Stone, in raising the problem of compliance with rules, are refe ring, not so much to informal processes arising within an admin trative structure, but to conditions outside the organization whi determine the members' orientations to the rules and the extent their consequent implementation.

'he view that administrative rationality cannot be assessed out of context of the culture in which an organization is situated has ɔme a standard item in the criticism of Max Weber, and is one he earliest critical comments to have been made. In 1928 a disuished German jurist, Rudolf Smend, complained that Weber responsible for the misconception that administration was a onal machine, and officials were mere technical functionaries. e judge and the administrative official are not *êtres inanimés*. ey are cultured (*geistig*), social beings, whose activity has a func- within a cultural whole. It is defined by that whole, is oriented ards it, and in return helps to define the nature of that whole.'[15] he light of this, he added, socialists were on sound ground when y complained of 'bourgeois justice'.

)ne of the clearest statements of the cultural limitations of ıinistrative rationality is contained in the work of Reinhard ıdix. He argues that the efficiency of an organization cannot be ssed without considering both its formal rules and human atti- es to them.[16] In his *Higher Civil Servants in American Society* 49) he argues against the belief that it is possible to adhere to a without the intrusion of general social and political values. All es have to be applied to particular cases, and in deciding whether ıse falls under a rule the official is called upon to make a judge- nt. In the exercise of his judgement the official is caught in a mma since 'too great a compliance with statutory rules is popu- y denounced as bureaucratic. Too great a reliance on initiative, rder to realize the spirit, if not the letter, of the law is popularly ıounced as an abuse of power, as interfering with legislative rogative'.[17]

The demonstration that rules can only be incomplete guides to ion not only implies that factors outside the rules must be taken ɔ account by the social scientist in interpreting the action of cials. It also highlights the necessity of choice with which every ninistrator is faced. It is held against Weber that he appears to mit his bureaucrat to elude all responsibility for his actions. He s either out of technical necessity or in accord with instructions. rl Friedrich criticizes Weber for this neglect of the notion of ponsibility. He holds that his emphasis on authority 'vibrates h something of the Prussian enthusiasm for the military type of anization, and the way seems barred to any kind of consultative, alone co-operative pattern'.[18] O. D. Corpuz makes a similar point and argues that responsibility stems from an adherence to titudes and values which are outside the administrative apparatu

Both those who, like Merton, delineate the unanticipated con quences of Weberian bureaucracy, and those who, like Bend stress that such a structure is contained within a larger socie agree in questioning the rationality and efficiency of Weber's id type. Other authors have approached Weber from another dir tion by asking themselves what, in a given situation, would co stitute rational administration, and then have gone on to comp their answers to this question with Weber's own. A good exam of such an approach is provided by Peter Blau's *The Dynamics Bureaucracy* (1955).

Blau considers the work of a United States federal law enfor ment agency and a state employment agency. In each he conce trates attention on the way formal regulations are implemented. the employment agency the central procedures for finding jobs the unemployed are modified locally in the interests of spee allocation of jobs. Statistical records of the officials' performance placing applicants in jobs are designed to permit comparat assessment and encourage competition between officials. Parado cally, Blau finds that a group of officials who co-operate with ea other and pay little attention to such assessments are more p ductive than those who are stimulated to competitiveness by t records. Even more striking is the way the persistent infringeme of a rule in the federal agency actually improves the chances achieving the agency's goal: the enforcement of two specific la relating to business finance. Officials who flout the rule that offers of bribes must be reported find that, by keeping the fact the offer to themselves (but not the money!), they can ensure t the businessman concerned co-operates fully, out of fear that attempted bribe will be reported.

The conclusion of Blau's thesis is that a fresh look has to be tak at the concept of rational administration. In a changing envirc ment, 'the stable attainment of organizational objectives deper on perpetual change in the bureaucratic structure'.[20] Therefo efficiency cannot be guaranteed by tethering the official to a set rigid rules. Only where he is allowed to identify with the purpo of the organization as a whole and to adapt his behaviour to perception of changing circumstances will efficient administrati result.

Similar conclusions to those of Blau have been drawn by A. L. nchcombe in an analysis of the American building industry.[21] argues that the occupational standards of the various craft titutions are the most efficient way of ensuring high quality ck. This factor and the great variability in the market in build- mean that certain features of Weber's concept of rational bur- cracy, such as continuity of administration, hierarchy and files not found in the construction industry. A similar argument has n applied to social welfare services. The needs of the poor or sick are held to demand something other than the Weberian del of administration.[22] Others insist that bureaucracy requires se ties with families and neighbourhoods before it can operate ciently in the modern community.[23]

Students of non-Western societies offer analogous arguments. us R. V. Presthus considers that Weber's concept of bureau- cy makes implicit assumptions about human motivation which not necessarily valid in non-Western environments. He finds t in the Turkish coal industry, economic and material incentives effort are not as effective as they would be in the West.[24] Delaney considers that patrimonial administration may well be re conducive to economic growth in under-developed societies n rational bureaucracy of the Weberian type.[25] J. La Palombara ws the same inference from a major collection of essays he s edited, *Bureaucracy and Political Development* (1963). He lieves that developing societies may find Russian or Chinese thods of administration more effective than Western bureau- cy.[26]

Weber believed that the growth of bureaucracy was inevitable. 'rationality' ensured it a place in the general process of rational- tion. Clearly this belief becomes questionable when, as with authors just cited, the very 'rationality' of bureaucracy itself is puted. But several writers go further and argue that, even if the ionality of Weber's ideal type is granted, this is no warrant for ing that it will always prevail over other administrative systems. us Gouldner has criticized the 'metaphysical pathos' of this sumption.[27] H. Constas accuses Weber of taking it for granted at the administrative staff of a charismatic movement will eventu- y be transformed into a legal bureaucracy.[28] R. Pipes rejects eber's interpretations of the Russian revolutions of 1905 and 17 and argues that he was far too impressed by the calibre of the imperial bureaucracy to be able to understand the potential o revolutionary movement.[29]

It is even suggested by H. G. Creel that Weber was mistal in seeing rational bureaucracy as a modern phenomenon, and tl almost all the characteristics of the ideal type existed in China 200 B.C.[30] Moreover, irrespective of any consideration of rationality of the ideal type, many writers consider that Wel erred in seeing it as the necessarily dominant administrative fo of the modern world. Thus A. B. Spitzer considers that functions of the nineteenth-century French prefect are far m comprehensive than those attributed to Weber's bureaucrat a represent a different tradition of administrative organizatior M. Berger on Egypt and C. Beck on Eastern Europe also obj to the proposition that non-Western administration is necessar tending in the direction of Weber's ideal type.[32]

One of the results of such criticisms has been a repeated eff to move away from what is regarded as the monolithic nature Weber's ideal type towards empirical research to find out j which characteristics do distinguish different administrative sy tems, and which are held in common. The simplest and m forceful statement of this point of view is contained in Carl Frie rich's "Some Observations on Weber's Analysis of Bureaucrac (1952).[33] He compares the central administrative bodies in Englar France, Prussia, the American colonies, and the United States. I finds six characteristics common to them: centralization of cont and supervision; differentiation of functions; qualification office; objectivity; precision and continuity; and secrecy. The features, he concludes, are essential to the concept of bureaucrac

Since Friedrich's essay several writers have emphasized that t characteristics of Weber's ideal type may each be regarded as variable. Thus a hierarchy of authority may exist to varying exte in different organizations, and it may or may not be accompani by selection procedures based on examinations. The inference drawn that administrative structures should be examined by me suring each of a variety of independently defined dimensio rather than from the standpoint of a unitary concept of burea cracy.[34] Such criticisms implicitly question the way Weber arriv at his formulation of the ideal type. Indeed many of the criticis discussed hitherto can be subsumed under a general criticism what is taken to be Weber's methodology.

The most succinct statement of the argument against Weber's thodology is contained in Blau and Scott's *Formal Organizations* 63): 'A careful reading of Weber indicates that he tends to view ments as "bureaucratic" to the extent that they contribute to ninistrative efficiency. This contribution to efficiency appears to the criterion of "perfect" embodied in the ideal type. However, ether or not each of these elements, or their combination, en- ices administrative efficiency is not a matter for definition; these questions of fact—hypotheses subject to empirical testing.'[35] In ier words, Weber is accused of offering a merely intuitive account what maximizes administrative efficiency.[36]

We may see that the foundations of such criticism were laid as ig ago as 1945 in a modern classic of administrative science, rbert Simon's *Administrative Behavior*. Without mentioning eber by name, Simon attacks those theorists who attempt to offer neless' principles of organizational efficiency. Simon argues that ferent situations require different administrative structures. nce the theorist's task is best construed as the refinement of the egories of thought appropriate to the diagnosis of administrative uations. In 1958, in his collaborative work with J. G. March and Guetskow, *Organisations*, Simon explicitly includes Weber ong the exponents of 'timeless' principles of administrative iciency.[37]

By now the reader can be in no doubt as to the formidable ture of the attack which has been mounted upon Weber's con- otualization of bureaucracy. The rationality of the ideal type is puted, both because of factors omitted from it, and because of ernal inconsistency. The degree of rationality it can have is held depend on the cultural context in which it is located. If it is cepted that rational bureaucracy is everywhere increasing, then is held that it must have different features from those which eber listed. Even if the rationality of Weber's ideal type is ac- pted, its inevitable growth is disputed. Finally, the very basis on ich Weber constructed the ideal type is held to be invalid.

A reply to the critics

If one wishes to sum up the nature of the disagreement be- een Weber and his critics it can be said that it has two themes. ne first is a dispute on the empirical validity (both historical and edictive) of his account of the nature and development of modern administration. The second, and more important, is a rejectior his association of the ideal type of bureaucracy with the concept rationality and efficiency. But such a statement of the second the begs an important question. Indeed, in order to remain as clos as possible to the position of the critics, it was deliberately beg throughout the last section. That question is: 'What did We mean by rationality and efficiency, and, in the context of bure cracy, can those terms be used interchangeably?'

When we turn to Weber's critics we find a general assumpt that when he spoke of rationality and bureaucracy, he was talk about efficiency. Certainly most of the writers cited in the section take it for granted that rationality meant for Weber suitability of means to a specific end. Thus Francis and Stone s 'By rationality Weber seems to mean that kind of action or mc of organizing in which goals are clearly conceived and all cond except that designed to achieve the particular goal is eliminated N. Mouzelis strikes a similar note: 'In the Weberian sense, ratio lity implies the appropriateness of means to ends. In the bure cratic context this means efficiency.'[39] A German sociolog sympathetic to Weber, Renate Mayntz, argues that the only re vant criticism of the ideal type must focus on the question whether it reaches maximum efficiency.[40]

This unanimity among the critics is especially surprising beca rationality is the most difficult and disputed of all the Weber concepts. Four major, and several minor variants of the conc occur repeatedly in his work, and they are conflated in his comp hensive developmental idea of rationalization. A general discussi of them would go beyond the scope of this work, but each of t major concepts of rationality appears at some point in Weber's d cussions of bureaucracy, and he makes several comments on t specific nature of rationality in a bureaucratic context.[41] It is these that we turn now.

Considerable time has been spent in showing the close aff ations between Weber's concept of bureaucracy and his oth organizational concepts. One facet of these was the link Web made between the pure type of bureaucracy and legal authori But it was not, it should be noted, the only form. (He made t clear in the eighth of his propositions on legal authority, see p. 4 This is a more important point than might at first appear to be t case. When Weber spoke of the rationality of legal authority it w because legal authority was necessarily associated with rational eaucracy. On the contrary, one of the reasons Weber called eaucracy rational was because it was a form of legal authority. : problem is thus raised of explaining why Weber attributed onality to legal authority.

Veber characterized the very conceptions of legitimacy which :ained legal authority as rational.[42] There were three reasons for . Such conceptions included the idea that both objectives and ıes could be formulated in a legal code.[43] Secondly, the abstract :s of the code were applied to specific cases, and administration olved the pursuit of interests within that framework.[44] Thirdly, duties of persons in such a system were limited to specific :s.[45] Weber called each one of these features rational. We can ount for this by considering two elements which appear in each :he three preceding features: the intention in the design of a e, and the procedure involved in the rule's application.

Veber termed rules 'rational' in so far as their intention was to p the achievement of purposes (technical rules) or to realize ıes (norms).[46] But the term 'rational' was not only appropriate ules because of the intention behind them. It could also be used designate the procedure of applying rules to particular cases. :h a procedure was, for Weber, intrinsically rational. Indeed in modern world it was becoming increasingly rational, so that it s necessary, both with technical rules and with norms, to employ alified men with the skill necessary to apply them.[47] It was this d of rationality which Weber had particularly in mind when he s discussing bureaucracy.

Two separate statements Weber made about the specific nature the rationality of bureaucracy support such an interpretation: ıreaucratic administration signifies authority on the basis of owledge. This is its specifically rational character';[48] and, 'Bur- cratic authority is specifically rational in the sense of being ınd to discursively analysable rules.'[49] Only if one realizes that ber regarded the implementation of rules in the modern organi- ion as a matter for the expert can one grasp the compatibility of se apparently divergent judgements. This procedure of expert olication of rules was central to what Weber called the *formal ionality* of bureaucracy.

t would be quite misleading to equate Weber's concept of formal ionality with the idea of efficiency. It certainly comprised techniques, such as accounting or filing. But it also meant legal ex tise, the interpretation of law by lawyers.[50] Administrative ac was not guided by technique alone, but also by norms. Moreo Weber frequently referred to the fact that formal rationality not guarantee what he called material rationality. Indeed the n perfect formal system might operate to defeat the purposes values which animated it.[51] This was, of course, implicit in recognition that bureaucrats might arrogate the highest positi in the state for themselves.

Formal rationality might be realized in either norms or te niques. But even technical formal rationality did not amoun efficiency. Certainly it implied calculability, predictability stability, but techniques were not in themselves sufficient to achi the purposes of an organization. Weber expressed himself ve mently on this point at a conference in Vienna in 1909. No denied, he argued, the 'technical superiority of the bureaucr machine'.[52] All were agreed that the high morality of the Gerr bureaucracy contributed to this superiority. But when it cam comparing the national power position of different countries German bureaucracy achieved far less than the corrupt machi of France and America. 'Which kind of organization has at moment the greatest "efficiency" (to use an English expression private capitalistic expansion, linked to a purely business officialde which is more easily open to corruption, or state direction un the highly moral, enlightened authoritarianism of the Gern officialdom?'[53]

This outburst is worthy of note not only because it shows t Weber was under no illusion that fine technique guaranteed eff ency. It also indicates that 'efficiency' was for him a foreign tern It appears in many translations of Weber's work but this refle more the preconceptions of the translator who cannot conceive rationality in the organization except as efficiency, than any c sistent usage by Weber of a term equivalent to efficiency.[55] In Weber's concept of formal rationality was more precise and sc ologically relevant than any connotation that might be attached the notoriously difficult idea of efficiency.[56]

If we define efficiency in a reasonably conventional way as ' attainment of a particular goal with the least possible detriment other goals', we can see that it corresponds with none of Webe categories of rationality. His idea of purposive rationality (*Zw onalitat*) can be seen as comprising efficiency, but it was more n that, involving series of ends and means. The real relation ween formal rationality and efficiency can best be understood considering the means by which efficiency is commonly meas- d, through the calculation of cost in money terms, or in time, n energy expended. Such calculations are formal procedures ch do not in themselves guarantee efficiency, but are among the ditions for determining what level of efficiency has been reached. he heart of Weber's idea of formal rationality was the idea of ect calculation, in either numerical terms, as with the account- or in logical terms, as with the lawyer. This was normally a essary though not sufficient condition for the attainment of ls; it could even conflict with material rationality.[57]

uch an interpretation must lead to the rejection of the charge lled at Weber that he attempted, on an intuitive basis, to state icient conditions for the attainment of any organizational goal. h of the propositions involved in his pure type of bureau- y referred to a procedure where either legal norms or monetary ulation were involved, and where impersonality and expert wledge were necessary. Any such procedure was for Weber insically rational, irrespective of its relation to organizational ctives. In short, he was not offering a theory of efficiency, but atement of the formal procedures which were prevalent in lern administration. In this sense Herbert Simon is quite cor- to point to the affinity between Weber's ideal type of bureau- y and the principles of the classical administrative theorists, he is quite wrong in assuming that Weber was subscribing to r principles.[58] On the contrary, as a sociologist Weber was rding what happened when men adhered to such theories.

his argument means also that criticism of Weber for neglecting cultural context of organizations misses the point. Indeed it be said that Weber was one step ahead of his critics in offering neral theory of modern culture. Where the values and beliefs society were informed by logic, calculation and scientific know- e, where, in other words, the rationalization process had ad- ced, there, argued Weber, bureaucracy could flourish. Rather viewing rational bureaucracy as an isolated social phenomenon, ber made it depend upon other formalized developments, in icular monetary calculation and legal codification.

hat do remain open to argument are the empirical validity of

Weber's characterization of modern administration and his pre
tions of its future development. But the argument must be regar
as evenly balanced. In many ways the formal rationality of mod
administration has increased. The features Weber picked out w
all exemplified in the Germany of his day. Most of them are t
of contemporary civil services. The growth of sciences of deci
making, of operational research, of schools of management amo
to an intensification of the importance of science in administra
—of formal rationality.[59]

On the other hand, it is undeniably true that he did not s
possible conflict between the growth of formal rules and the ap
cation of scientific knowledge. Indeed modern emphasis on
necessity of giving experts a free hand, on flexibility in adminis
tion, on job enlargement, on increasing discretion, runs counte
Weber's predictions of ever-increasing formalization. Nor is it
dom after the event to point this out. Weber's own brother, Alf
was already writing in 1910 of the need to transform work in
means of personal fulfilment, and was predicting that men wo
eventually find that the excessively tight bonds of bureaucr
organization were unnecessary.[60]

To conclude, one may say that the novel, unique, and, for l
commentators, disturbing feature of Max Weber's account of b
eaucracy was his utter disregard for the problems of efficiency.
is this surprising. In a theory of the special nature of Western c
lization the problems which concerned men such as Olszev
could only appear trivial.[61] Perhaps, given a greater interest in s
issues, Weber might have considered the importance Mill
placed upon tradition in maintaining efficiency. He might e
have modified the inflexible nature of his predictions to fit
brother's vision. We have seen that he did question the efficie
of German bureaucracy. But, however much he had been c
cerned with this problem, he would never have needed to ret
his view that modern bureaucracy involved *formal* rationality.

4/Bureaucracy and the Ideologists

Max Weber's work was the culmination of the attempt to ach the idea of bureaucracy from the polemical context in which ad emerged. But this did not mean that the concept of bureau- cy was deprived of its place in political controversy. Weber him- attacked the German bureaucracy while, at the same time, mpting to maintain a strict separation between polemics and ached political analysis. Since his time the gap between aca- nic and polemical treatment of the problem of bureaucracy has lened still further. Denunciations of bureaucracy and academic erest in the topic are absorbing the energies of distinct groups of sons, let alone being maintained as separate spheres within the ivities of an individual.

n such circumstances some justification for paying even slight ntion to the concept of bureaucracy in ideological contexts ears to be necessary. Three reasons can be offered. In the first ce, while ideologies are designed to incite men to action this does mean that their content is wholly emotive. On the contrary, it is ature of modern ideologies that they purport to be based upon objective view of the nature of man and society. Secondly, it is oriously difficult for the social scientist to remove all traces of ological commitment from his own work, and it is therefore im- tant to be aware of the nature of ideological concepts of bureau- cy. Thirdly, Marxist, and to a lesser extent Fascist, ideologies m to erase the distinction between ideological and scientific king, at least as far as their own doctrines are concerned. Poli- l leaders set themselves up as arbiters of scientific truth and demics avowedly direct their work to political ends. That the ntific element in this conflation of ideology and knowledge can- be lightly disregarded is obvious when we consider the high stige as a political scientist which Karl Marx, the most successful logist of all time, has in non-Marxist circles.

Karl Marx

In spite of the prolific nature of his writing, Marx m more than passing reference to bureaucracy in one essay only, first important work after his dissertation, the *Kritik des Hegels Staatsrechts*. This was written in 1843, yet, despite its importa it was not published until 1927.[1] In consequence Marxist dis sions of bureaucracy depend on inferences drawn from Ma general political philosophy rather than his specific analysis of subject. As we shall see such inferences have been fraught v problems, and it could well be that Marx's neglect of the sub stemmed from a perception that his early analysis of bureaucr fitted badly into his economic interpretation of politics.

Marx introduced the idea of bureaucracy into his criticism Hegel's conception of the executive powers of the state. In *Philosophy of Right* (1821), Hegel advanced the view that the s was the vehicle of a general interest distinct from the separate particular interest of the members of civil society. It was the tas the executive to implement decisions (made by the monarch) ab the nature of this general interest. It was shared between colle advisory committees and state officials and conducted accordin the principle of the division of labour, specific duties being a cated to separate departments hierarchically organized un ministers. Since it could not be assumed that any individual endowed by nature with the ability to execute the general inter officials had to be specially educated for their task and financi supported so that their personal interests never interfered with objective fulfilment of their duties.

Hegel singled out two factors for their importance in ensu that the actions of officials did not exceed the bounds of the gen interest. The first was the system of hierarchic authority. second was the independence of corporations and local comm ties which embodied the special interests of particular so groups. But, in addition to these formal factors, he held that values and attitudes of the officials themselves were imbued wi sense of justice and selflessness. The officials made up the m important part of the middle class in which the honesty intelligence needed by the modern state was concentrated.[2]

Marx's criticism of this account was scathing: Hegel's works not deserve to be called philosophical exposition, for most of w ıad to say could have appeared word for word in the Prussian al code. He was simply discussing bureaucracy. It is important note that Marx introduced the term *Bureaucratie* and did not e it from Hegel's text. As one commentator has pointed out, ırx was using it in a pejorative sense.[3] It referred to all the ele- nts in the hierarchical system of administration Hegel outlined, n the collegial advisory boards. In Marx's usage it could refer h to the system of administration and to the men who implemen- that system, but more frequently to the latter. If it was the latter had more in mind he often simply spoke of 'the bureaucrats'.[4]

Marx objected fundamentally to the way Hegel examined the ationship between state and society. In the first place they were arated, the state representing the general interest, society being de up of special interests, and then they were reunited through devices of hierarchy, independent rights for corporations and high morality of the official. This appeared to Marx a completely torted picture. The theoretical opposition between general and cial interests was illusory and was used by the bureaucrats to tify their own special interest. Each of the mechanisms Hegel arded as ensuring the unity of state and society merely evidenced conflict between the two. The paper qualifications of the bur- ıcrat were a mark of his separation from the rest of society, the e purposes of the state were submerged in secrecy, mechanistic ion, faith in authority and the quest for higher positions in the rarchy. 'In bureaucracy the identity of the interests of state and the particular private purpose is so established that the interests state become a particular private purpose confronting other vate purposes.'[5]

Marx agreed with Hegel that the bureaucrats were the main lar of a middle class, but asked what sort of organization could it ve if it depended on a balance of conflicting interests of the cials and other specially privileged groups. The executive wer belonged to the whole people and this could only happen en special interest had genuinely become the interest of all.

The section devoted to bureaucracy constituted an important t of the *Kritik des Hegelschen Staatsrechts*. It was a topic on ich Marx had clearly thought deeply. But thereafter he scarcely ve it any attention. He made occasional mention of the bureau- ıts, but the *Kritik* was neither cited nor published and the ırxist theory of the state developed in independence of it. We

must briefly consider Marx's theory of the state if we wish
understand why he allowed the concept of bureaucracy to drop i
such an obscure place in his work.

In *The German Ideology* (1846), Marx asserted that although
state had become a separate entity it was 'nothing more than
form of organisation which the bourgeois necessarily adopt . . .
the mutual guarantee of their property and interests'.[6] In the *Ma*
festo of the Communist Party (1848), he interpreted political pov
as 'merely the organised power of one class for oppressing anothe
In the *Critique of the Gotha Programme* (1875), he criticized
shallowness of socialist ideas which could not see that existi
society was the basis of the existing state and failed to understa
that the state was not 'an independent entity that possesses its o
intellectual, ethical, and libertarian bases'.[8]

Even where, as in *The German Ideology*, Marx appeared to all
the state a separate identity, he rapidly insisted that this indepe
dence was illusory. Throughout his career he attacked libera
anarchists and socialists alike for believing that either the reform
abolition of the state amounted to a sensible proposition. Since
state depended on the class structure, only a revolution whi
swept that structure away could effect real political change.
showed particular animosity towards Karl Heinzen, whose stu
of Prussian bureaucracy appeared two years after Marx's critic
of Hegel's position. 'The fatuous Heinzen,' he wrote, 'connecti
the existence of classes with the existence of *political* privileges a
monopolies.'[9]

Could it be that Marx reacted so vehemently against Heinz
precisely because that author had drawn implications from burea
cracy which Marx himself had been perilously near to doing in
own discussion? In it bureaucracy appeared as a near autonomo
force, developing its own mode of existence, ruling the rest
society in its own interests.[10] It was a direction of argument whi
Marx, in developing the idea of the state as the organized power
economically based classes, could not afford to pursue. Bureaucra
had to be seen as an appendage. Any suggestion that the body whi
merely implemented the formal arrangements of government cou
become a determining influence on the future of society wou
have run counter to the belief that nothing could prevent econon
forces producing the polarization of society into bourgeoisie a
proletariat.

But what sort of appendage was bureaucracy? The insignificant ıce to which Marx relegated the concept of bureaucracy after his ·ly discussion in the *Kritik* barely concealed the analytical prob- ı with which he was faced. In *The German Ideology* he saw reaucracy arising in the German states and acquiring abnormal lependence because of the inability of any interest group to minate the others. This transitional stage had persisted in ·rmany longer than elsewhere, but even so, fundamentally it was : interests of the bourgeoisie which were being served.[11] Yet, ly three years later, Marx was saying that the Prussian liberal vernment of 1848, installed after the March insurrection in rlin, was representative of the bourgeoisie and had to replace the l bureaucracy 'which does not wish to sink to the level of ıidservant to a bourgeoisie to which it was once despotic ıoolmistress'.[12]

In *The Eighteenth Brumaire of Louis Bonaparte* (1852), Marx nsidered that the mass of peasant smallholders in France pro- led a very suitable base for bureaucracy. With no intermediate ades between it and government direct interference of state wer was called forth.[13] Louis Bonaparte was 'forced to create an ıificial caste, for which the maintenance of his regime becomes a ead-and-butter question'.[14] This regime was representative of e peasant masses, but at the same time it safeguarded bourgeois der. Not surprisingly Marx noted that this situation was full of ntradictions'.

Thus, in spite of detecting the existence of bureaucracy in differ- t societies, serving different classes, Marx refused to give it any ore than a passing significance. He did not see it as posing any oblem for society after the proletarian revolution. In the *Mani- to of the Communist Party*, he envisaged the proletariat centraliz- g production, credit, means of communication and transport in e hands of the state prior to the 'public power losing its political aracter'.[15] In *The Civil War in France* (1871), the most impor- nt source for his views on the future shape of political power, he sumed that it would be possible for all administrative positions be filled by election and that their incumbents would be truly sponsible to self-governing communes. Since bureaucracy was a ıss instrument, in a classless society it would not exist—a perhaps t too simple summary of Marx's position.

There can be no question, as is sometimes suggested, that Marx neglected the idea of bureaucracy simply because he was not ab any more than any one else in his time, to foresee twentieth-cent developments. His own contemporaries criticized him on t issue. Bakunin, the Russian anarchist who struggled with Marx control of the International Workingmen's Association, conside that every state was necessarily based upon military and bureauc tic centralization. He criticized Marx and his followers for refusi to see that their ideas were bound to lead to a minority of ex-work ruling the masses in a powerfully centralized state.[16]

But it was not the anarchists alone who made an issue of bure cracy. It was a theme which had the unique capacity of uniti conservative, liberal and socialist critics of nineteenth-cent social trends. Marx's neglect of it was a pointed effort to dissoci himself from all other ideologies of his time. It affected even rem areas of his historical studies. Karl Wittfogel has shown how Mar study of Oriental societies was distorted by his refusal to ackno ledge that the bureaucracy constituted the ruling class where th was total state power.[17] It was a refusal which was to have d consequences for later Marxists.

The later Marxists

The lacunae in Marx's account of bureaucracy present his successors with a double problem. In the first place, they h very little guidance as to how a revolutionary party, and, afte revolution, a socialist state, should be organized. Secondly, onc socialist state had been established the emergence of features in t administrative system which seemed to resemble much which w condemned as bureaucracy in bourgeois states had no easy the etical explanation. The full brunt of both sides of this problem v met by Lenin. His attempts to resolve the problem met w opposition at every stage.

Lenin's genius resided in his capacity both to organize and theorize about organization. He was convinced that rational orga ization was necessary both for winning power and for at least t early stages of a socialist society. At the same time he had demonstrate his rights to leadership by expounding Marxi ideology. Marx's rejection of bureaucracy as an instrument of cl rule clearly hindered him in his organizational task. Before t revolution of 1917 Lenin tried on occasions to eliminate the p orative connotations of bureaucracy. In 1904 he asserted that volutionary party had to be based upon formal, 'bureaucratically' rded rules, and he even called bureaucracy 'the organisational inciple of revolutionary Social Democracy'.[18] It was as a result of putes about such tactics that the split occurred at the party con- ss of 1903 between Lenin's own group, which became known the Bolsheviks, and those who were out-voted, the Mensheviks. But Lenin's insistence upon regulations and discipline was not nply arguable on tactical grounds. Its ideological basis in arxism was also dubious. The German revisionist leader, luard Bernstein, had already warned that the great danger inher- t in revolution was the breeding of bureaucracy and he empha- ed those aspects of Marx's teaching which implied the necessity r elaborate self-government.[19] Rosa Luxemburg quarrelled rectly with Lenin, accusing him of wanting to enslave a young bour movement to an intellectual élite by means of a bureaucratic rait-jacket.[20] She remained of this opinion even after the Russian evolution. She criticized the lack of freedom of speech, the sence of elections and the right of free assembly. The bureau- acy alone remained as an active element in the state.[21] A different ne of attack came from a former ally, Karl Kautsky, who wanted accept the principle of the inevitability of bureaucratic organiza- on, and wished to re-direct the existing state machinery in the terests of the workers.[22]

Lenin's most ambitious attempt to answer these contradictory iticisms simultaneously was contained in *The State and the evolution* (1917). On the one hand he asserted that the old state achinery had to be smashed. On the other he insisted on the ecessity for strong central control, a dictatorship of the proletariat hich would precede the withering away of the state. The burden f his argument was to emphasize that the new form of state insti- uted after the revolution would be quite distinct from that which ent before. There would be government, but it would be in the ands of the armed proletariat. Representative institutions would xist, but not as bourgeois parliamentarianism. They would be Soviets f workers and soldiers deputies. There would be officials, but they ould not become bureaucrats, 'i.e., privileged persons divorced om the people and standing *above* the people. That is the *essence* f bureaucracy.'[23]

In order to distinguish his position from Kautsky's, Lenin was orced to refine his idea of bureaucracy. Kautsky had a 'superstitious belief' in it because he failed to understand that, while str discipline and utmost precision were demanded in all mode organizations, it was not necessary for them to be exercised appointed officials with power and privilege. So Lenin dissociat his own organizational principles from the idea of bureaucracy, a entrusted their realization to a new, proletarian administrati apparatus. This was to be based on the lessons Marx found in t Paris Commune of 1871. Workers deputies were to supervise t management of the apparatus. They were to be elected, and subje to recall. Their pay was not to exceed a worker's. There was to 'immediate introduction of control and supervision by *all*, so th *all* may become "bureaucrats" for a time and that, therefor *nobody* may be able to become a "bureaucrat" '.[24]

If there were any tendencies for proletarian functionaries to b come bureaucrats, Lenin attributed them to the corruptive co ditions of capitalism. Until the bourgeoisie had been overthrow there was bound to be some degree of bureaucratization.[25] Sma though this reservation was, it took on enormous significance aft the revolution. For the issue of bureaucracy rapidly became th focus of the grievances of dissident groups. Under the crisis co ditions of the post-revolutionary period, Lenin's programme fo proletarian administration was far from being realized. The Nint Party Congress of 1920 heard scathing attacks on 'bureaucrati centralism'.[26] The Kronstadt sailors' revolt of 1921 listed th bureaucratization of the party as one of the dissidents' majo reasons for discontent.[27] At the Tenth Congress, the Worker Opposition under Alexandra Kollontai demanded a programme o reform which included the expulsion of non-proletarian elemen from administration, elections to administrative positions, and th suppression of bureaucracy in the party.[28]

Lenin had to admit that the old state apparatus had not bee smashed. At the Eleventh Party Congress he conceded the insuf ficiencies of Soviet administration, but he would not attribute thes to his own organizational principles. Bureaucracy was a survival from the pre-revolutionary period.[29] It was a line to which Stali tenaciously adhered. In 1925 he admitted that there was a dange of the party losing control of the state apparatus. But this was th result of bourgeois influence, and the state was quite distinct fron bourgeois government since it served the interests of the proletariat In his report to the Sixteenth Congress of the Communist Party i

30 Stalin conceded that there might even be a new type of mmunist bureaucrat who stifled the working class with decrees, d he announced a plan to 'cleanse the apparatus'.[30] In the 1940s e Soviet campaign against bureaucratic tendencies continued in e same vein. Capitalist encirclement and bourgeois survivals were ld to contribute to superciliousness and negligence in government and party officials.[31]

Whatever judgement is made on the practicality of the antithesis bureaucracy which Lenin formulated in *The State and the volution*, it did mark an advance in sophistication in Marxist inking about administration. In the harsh years which followed was largely ignored. The rules of poverty and recall for officials ere abrogated.[32] 'Bureaucracy', instead of being a key term in a eory of administration, became an abusive catchword. Ironically usage signified an attitude equivalent to that found in nineteenth-ntury states and heavily criticized by Marx. 'Ultimately, because ery state attributes its weaknesses to accidental or intentional fects in administration, it looks to administrative measures to ovide the remedy. Why? Precisely because administration is the ganising activity of the state.'[33] Marx was arguing that only the struction of the class system would provide a genuine solution. talin was the last person to want to pursue the implications of such line of thought.

But if, inside Russia, Marxist thinking on bureaucracy was stulfied, outside, Marxist opponents of Soviet policy found disturbg theoretical problems in the practices of the Stalinist state. The cts of power in Russia, the fact that the withering away of the ate seemed more and more unlikely, appeared to be contrary to me basic tenets, namely: that the sequence of changes through fferent types of society was determinate; that types of society ere deduced from class structure; that politics reflected class ructure. How could Russian politics possibly be explained in ese terms? The most influential writer to consider this question as Leon Trotsky.

Lenin and Trotsky quarrelled over the latter's criticism of the owth of bureaucracy, and this issue precipitated Trotsky's break ith Stalin.[34] In 1924 he criticized the way the party apparatus was nbued with a feeling of its own importance and he lamented that eninism had become a sacred canon rather than something emanding initiative and ideological courage.[35] In *The Revolution*

Betrayed (1937), he considered the theoretical implications of t emergence of a privileged and commanding stratum in the Sovi Union, the bureaucracy. Trotsky had no doubt that it was legi mate to call the privileged officials of party and government Russia by the same name as the administrative officials of bou geois societies. Russian officials were also concerned to mainta a system of social ranks; they too exploited the state for their ow ends. But there was a crucial difference. 'The Soviet bureaucra takes on bourgeois customs without having beside it a nation bourgeoisie.'[36]

The crucial question for Marxist theory was whether such bureaucracy constituted a ruling class. Although Trotsky reco nized that it controlled the means of production, he considere that it lacked the essential and distinctive feature of a class: special type of property. The bureaucracy was, therefore, a stratu or caste, parasitic upon socialist society. Soviet Russia did n require a social revolution, as in 1917, but merely a political revolu tion which would oust the bureaucracy without changing the basi form of social relations. Hence it was not a new type of society, bu was poised between the bourgeois and socialist types.

Trotsky stopped short of a clear break with the orthodox Marxis sequence of societal types. Others were not so timid. A little know work by Bruno Rizzi, *La Bureaucratisation du Monde* (1939) explicitly took issue with Trotsky.[37] Rizzi argued that a new clas had arisen in the Soviet Union since the bureaucracy, by payin itself high salaries, became the owner of the surplus value produce by the proletariat. The existence of the new class justified talkin of a new type of society which Rizzi designated 'bureaucrati collectivist'. Credit for developing this concept was also claime by Max Schachtman, editor of *The New International*, who, in a series of articles in that journal from 1940 onwards, rejected th notion that the Soviet Union was either socialist or capitalist.[38]

Schachtman disagreed with those who thought modern societies were converging to a managerial type. He thus indicated his independence from a line of thought of which Rizzi was an early exponent. For the latter found that the United States and Fascist societies were equally dominated by professional specialists and technicians.[39] All developed societies were approaching an identical destiny and Marxists were deluded in thinking that the proletariat could ever obtain power without generating bureaucracy. None e less Rizzi believed that the skill of the bureaucrats would entually raise the material conditions of life to the point where e gap between them and the working classes would be minimal.[40] ch an approach, which emphasized the role of specialist know-lge in both government and the economy, highlighted specific tures of the twentieth century which necessarily strained tradi-nal Marxist analysis.

The most celebrated and most radical departure from that alysis came in 1957 with the publication of *The New Class* by ilovan Djilas, former vice-president of Yugoslavia. It is well own that this book occasioned a seven-year prison sentence, but theoretical significance has been neglected. At point after point jilas breaks with basic Marxist tenets. Communist states are run the party. The party is a bureaucracy. The bureaucracy is a class ce it uses and disposes of state property. But it also depends on o other equally important factors; force and ideological dogma-m. It needs these to secure its power precisely because it is not mly embedded in the socio-economic order. It is not a transi-nal phenomenon, but part of a special type of state system. This stem will develop in separate national directions.

Certainly the mere fact of an attack on bureaucracy did not danger Djilas. In 1949 and 1950 Tito was leading attacks on the viet state system and criticizing Stalin for bureaucratic tenden-es. A programme was implemented to secure decentralization and ntrol at all levels by people's committees.[41] But, as I. Lapenna inted out, the place of the conception of bureaucracy in Soviet d Yugoslav theory did not vary greatly.[42] In both cases attention as concentrated on what were seen to be remediable administra-ve abuses, even though the practical measures differed. Djilas's tack was designed to subvert the whole Communist theory of the ate. It was more dangerous by far than a programme of adminis-ative reform.

Outside Europe, where revolutionary movements with a Marxist eology have taken control, the same ambivalences towards the lea of bureaucracy as appeared in the Soviet Union are apt to cur. Mao Tse-tung regularly fuses the ideas of bureaucracy and pitalism and attacks 'bureaucrat-capitalists'.[43] He also refers to e dangers of bureaucracy in the Communist Party, but he warns gainst equating counter-revolutionary bureaucracy with the revo-tionary form, which is a correctable malady. Similarly, in Cuba

Castro has attacked the socialist bureaucrats in his own agenci
But, as a sympathetic outsider, René Dumont, has commented, t
Cuban leaders regard bureaucratic tendencies as a mysterio
disease, cause unknown.[44] For the more romantic 'Che' Gueva
such issues were merely 'quantitative' and ultimately of lit
importance.[45]

Only in the last few years, with the rise of the diffuse moveme
known as the New Left, has the concept of bureaucracy come
take a major place in doctrine which claims to stem from Mar
Lichtheim has pointed out that the Hungarian rising of 19
secured the admission from critically minded Marxists th
bureaucracy was the central problem for the new society.[46] T
spokesmen of the Paris student revolt of May, 1968, bear out th
judgement. One of them goes as far as to define socialism as 'a reje
tion of all bureaucracy, of all centralized direction, by granting pow
to the producers at their point of production'.[47] But their idea
bureaucracy is more all-embracing than that of even the ear
Marx. It appears to comprise hierarchy, specialization, authori
and alienation. Such a concept is derived as much from the multipl
factor approach of modern sociology as from Marx, and so acute
the consciousness of the Procrustean nature of modern organiz
tion that any structuring of the student movement is rejected f
fear of the taint of bureaucracy.[48]

Probably a turning point in left-wing ideology has been reache
More conventional Marxists of the New Left, for instance tho
who contributed to the *May Day Manifesto 1968*, may avoid a fu
confrontation with the problem of bureaucracy, but the stude
activists in France or the United States have made organization
structure, rather than the class system, their main target.[49] Th
systematization of these ideas requires an ideologist with as muc
knowledge of modern social and political science as Marx had
bourgeois philosophy and economics. Kautsky and Djilas a
merely notable exceptions to the rule that, hitherto, Marxists hav
shunned Western social science.[50]

Whether such an ideological synthesis would generate new poli
tical forms is an issue which cannot be pursued here. But it i
noteworthy that a theoretical dispute over bureaucracy has so ofte
been the ostensible reason for many famous partings of the way i
the Communist world—between the Bolsheviks and Menshevik
Trotsky and Stalin, Stalin and Tito, Tito and Djilas. An ideolog

ith a developed doctrine of bureaucracy would at least be spared obvious pretext for schism. In this respect, Fascism provides an structive example.

The Fascists

As opposed to the Marxists, the Fascists not only put a eory of the state at the centre of their doctrine, they also sought resolve the problem of the relation of the individual to the state asserting the identity of their interests. Authority, hierarchy, edience were extolled, and even if attempts were made to capitae on the unpopularity of civil servants, Fascists were too intent capturing the state intact and using it for their own ends to be le to afford to alienate its instruments. Their ideology was, erefore, unique in its response to bureaucracy. It was not condered to present any problem, and the term itself lost any jorative connotations.[51]

However, in comparison with Marxism, Fascist ideology was a rgely *ad hoc* collection of ideas assembled for opportunistic asons.[52] It was, therefore, conditioned very directly by the cirmstances in which its was conceived, and it would be wrong to eglect the differing emphases placed on the idea of bureaucracy Italy and Germany. The Italian Fascists had the problem of stering greater docility to state interference, while the Nazis had re-direct an already highly developed state machine. Hence for Iussolini: 'It is not the nation which generates the State . . . rather is the State which creates the nation',[53] while for Hitler, 'the tate is not an end but a means', drawing its strength from the ation and merely helping to promote its development.[54]

Mussolini made a point of praising the Italian state officials as ften as possible. In a speech in 1924 he said that the bureaucracy one had prevented chaos in Italy.[55] In his autobiography he serted: 'All that is just, finds in the Italian bureaucracy an imediate comprehension.'[56] In a speech on the corporate state, in 933, he denied that bureaucracy was any barrier between the eople and the state since, under Fascism, the citizen was intimatey associated with the administrative machinery.[57] Mussolini dmired the machinery of state because it was on similar principles hat he had built his own party, and the society he envisaged was be based on interlocking hierarchies.[58] He saw bureaucracy simly as a body of officials or the method of modern administration, a fact of modern life to be taken for granted. It was a formulati strikingly similar to that of his admirer, Michels. Only when spoke of bureaucratization, the freezing of the economy und communism, did a disparaging tone enter his comments.[59]

The idea of bureaucracy had an insignificant place in Na writing. Hitler asserted that his movement would put life in machine when he spoke of the civil service of the Weimar Republi but he expressed admiration for the competence and incorrupt bility of the civil service of the empire.[60] He could not afford disparage the force, which, next to the army, was the most powe ful in the state. At the same time, when he came to power he trie to ensure its subservience to himself by subjecting it to Na supervision and infiltration. The consequences of this have frequen ly been analysed by later commentators, but at the time ideologic justification was perfunctory.[61] Alfred Rosenberg wrote once c twice of the way German officialdom had been brought out of th bureaucrat's office and given back to the people, but the Nazis fe little need of any more elaborate theory.[62]

The fact that a dispassionate concept of bureaucracy as a instrument of the state was held both in Fascist thought and in th theories of the classical writers, and the fact that these were th productions of the same two countries, could occasion an over simple linking of the two sets of ideas. In the case of Michels link can be made, but to say that, by analogy, the link must be ther also between Weber and Nazism would be to neglect the specifi features of the Nazi ideology. For it is clear from a leading aca demic sympathizer with Hitler, Carl Schmitt, that Weber's idea c bureaucracy could not appeal to a movement which claimed t revitalize the nation. Hitler needed the bureaucracy as an instru ment but also as a political ally prepared to intervene in nationa life in a direct way on his behalf. Weber, argued Schmitt, neglecte the role of bureaucracies as élites and carriers of values and coul only see them as purely technical bodies.[63]

If the Nazis supported bureaucracy it was because they saw in i an élite group prepared to assist them in exercising power. Fo them and the Italian Fascists this represented the intimate unio of nation and state. It is precisely these connotations of bureaucracy, a privileged élite group claiming to represent nationa interests, which has been the target of ideologists committed t Western representative institutions.

The ideologists of representative democracy

A good illustration of the limitations of the concepts of right d left wing is provided by the attitudes of Western conservatives d socialists towards bureaucracy. Although those who do not ish to see existing social inequalities undermined might be con-dered to be on the same wing as the Fascists, their views on reaucracy are diametrically opposite. Similarly the socialist mmitted to Western representative institutions tends to accept reaucracy as a fact of modern life and does not share the larxist's antipathy towards it.

In the United States especially, and to a lesser extent in Britain, nservatism has been associated with opposition to governmental tervention, and it has become customary to attack all such activity bureaucracy. A large literature exists which singles out for attack ecific features of government and labels them 'bureaucracy'.[64] uch features may be the proliferation of regulations or the opposite, e bestowal of discretion upon the official, or nationalization, or fficials who behave obnoxiously, or sometimes simply socialism. lerring has commented on this genre of writing and its use of the oncept of bureaucracy. He argues that 'bureaucracy' has become n emotional stereotype meaning only 'that-aspect-of-administra-on-which-is-disliked-by-those-who-are-adversely-affected'.[65]

The nearest approach to a measured exposition of the conserva-ve concept of bureaucracy is in the work of Ludwig von Mises. rguing that the term always has opprobrious connotations he sserts that 'nobody has ever tried to determine in unambiguous nguage what bureaucracy really means'.[66] This comment is a ood illustration of the intellectual isolation of the exponents of this oncept of bureaucracy. Von Mises ignores virtually all the previ-us literature on bureaucracy—and understandably so—since he ries to show that inefficiency is of the essence of governmental ntervention, and that it is only governmental inefficiency which leserves the name of bureaucracy. Indeed he argues that private nterprise only shows the traits of bureaucracy as a result of public nterference. Bureaucracy is the antithesis of business motivated y the desire for profit. It is the same conflict as that between apitalism and socialism.

Von Mises is both attacking socialists and trying to forestall their ustomary rejoinder, which is that all modern organizations, public or private, show essentially the same traits. Socialists reject t concept of bureaucracy as governmental interference and rea with some degree of fatalism to what they regard as the univers features of modern organization: size, impersonality, regulatio Thus Schumpeter confesses: 'I for one cannot visualize, in t conditions of modern society, a socialist organization in any for other than that of a huge and all embracing bureaucratic apparatu Every other possibility I can conceive would spell failure a breakdown.'[67] But he goes on to argue that bureaucracy affec every sphere of life, and that it is a necessary complement modern democracy.

Schumpeter also suggests the conditions under which burea cracy can work to the advantage of democracy. But such conce for this problem is rare among socialists.[68] Normally it is mentione in passing only. Among British Labour Party politicians on Richard Crossman has shown a consistent desire to specify t mechanisms which could abate the problems of a swelling civ service, the concentration of power in public and private corpora tions, the growing independence of the civil servant. His collectio of essays, *Planning for Freedom* (1965), emphasizes the necessity power with responsibility, the need for Parliamentary committee and further constitutional safeguards for individual citizens.

The only group in recent British politics which has attempted make bureaucracy a central issue of controversy has been th Liberal Party. It has advocated workers' control in industry an called for the devolution of government functions. Its forme leader, Jo Grimond, has expressed admiration for Yugoslav re forms of the last decade, and in many respects the party has pu sued a line of thought very similar to that of the more unorthodo Marxists of the New Left. In both cases the concept of burea cracy embraces the whole area of contact between individual an organization. In Grimond's words: 'In saying that our system "bureaucratic" I mean primarily that decisions tend to be take by the pressure of various organizations acting in the interests their own apparatus. Anyone outside an organization is of litt importance.'[69]

As we shall see, the preoccupations of the British Liberals ru approximately parallel to those of many contemporary politica scientists. Yet it is difficult to conceal the fact that the total fund o ideas on bureaucracy possessed by Western politicians seem arse, even when compared with the Marxists'. This must be tributed to the very division of labour between scientist and litician which the Marxist aims to abolish. It is a presupposition the ideology of representative democracy that the academic udy of political life can be pursued without endangering, indeed en without relevance to, accepted political institutions.

But the idea of bureaucracy has rarely been divorced from the eling that it involves practical problems which demand solutions. any Western academics do conceive it as their task to offer 'solu-ons' to the problem of bureaucracy. They aim to act as brokers tween the politician and the scientist, interpreting the meaning democracy for the latter, giving the facts to the former. They ay, perhaps, be viewed as the real ideologists and we shall con-der them in chapter 6. Before that we must turn to that peculiar oduct of the West, the continuing attempt to develop an objec-ve, dispassionate, detached account of a controversial political pic—in short, social science.

5/Seven Modern Concepts of Bureaucracy

It is possible a reader will turn with relief to this chapt hoping that the plethora of competing concepts previously detail will finally be clarified and organized. He may have interpreted t purpose of the earlier chapters as the provision of a backcloth definitive achievements by the present generation of scholars. B if so, he will be disappointed. For, as the mention of seven concep of bureaucracy implies, modern endeavour in the social scienc has led to a further proliferation of concepts. Sophistication in arg ment and research has not resolved old problems, but mere elaborated them, and the relation of the earlier chapters to this o is more in the nature of an explanation of the basic positions fro which modern argument stems than a foretaste of better things come.

As with any argument, if one comes in at a late stage a pr requisite for understanding how that stage has been reached is retrace the course of discussion, and this is true even if those wh are arguing are no longer aware of how they have reached the present positions. In this way, some sense can be found in a sit ation where literally hundreds of definitions of bureaucracy con pete and where the differences between them amount to more tha minor verbal discrepancies. For this reason modern concepts bureaucracy will be classified here according to their historical an logical affiliations with the concepts which have already bee examined. Such a procedure recommends itself all the more clear since it has already been followed, and in part completed, in respe of the continuing debates with Weber and within Marxism. Only this way can any thematic unity behind modern concepts bureaucracy be discerned.

The discussion in this chapter does not follow the only possib mode of presentation. Several alternative modes present themselve If one wished to highlight the fragmentation of the literature would be sufficient to present concepts of bureaucracy according disciplinary affiliation of the authors. Historians, political ntists, economists, management scientists, sociologists and ial psychologists have, in general, preferred to discuss differing cepts of bureaucracy within their own discipline rather than to k for similar concepts in other disciplines.

t would also be possible to consider concepts of bureaucracy ording to the types of general propositions with which they ght be associated. Bureaucracy has normally been a term in a le variety of theories about modern society. It has been linked h the growth of tertiary occupations, with the differentiation of ial functions, with the alienation of man from work, with the wth of oligarchy and with a general process of rationalization. It been an element in many more restricted theories about rules, rarchy, communication, participation and decision making in a le variety of organizations. But there has been no consistent king of particular concepts of bureaucracy with particular ories. Thus, while some theorists may agree on employing the cept of bureaucracy in the sense of the power of officials, they quite likely to disagree on whether the growth of such power is be anticipated in industrialized societies. Others may agree that growth of formal regulations is likely to hinder free communion but disagree as to whether such formal regulation is to be led bureaucracy. Another possibility is that ostensibly similar positions may be advanced: e.g. that bureaucracy increases the elihood of alienation from work, when in one case a writer is ing bureaucracy to mean a rational system of organization, and another case administrative inefficiency is what is meant.

This does not amount to saying that the choice of concept has no plications at all for the kind of theories a social scientist may vance. We have seen, for instance, how the concepts of bureaucy held by Mosca, Michels and Weber were part of a conceptual me of reference which tended to exclude the possibility of formung generalizations about administrative inefficiency. We shall e such limiting tendencies again. But to view concepts primarily m the standpoint of the theories of which they form elements, indeed, of the disciplines in which they have been elaborated, uld involve separate analyses of the development of those ories or disciplines.

The same might be said of a third way in which the ensuing dission might be organized; that is, according to the conceptual strategy which the various writers have employed. The very fac variety among concepts of bureaucracy confronts social scient with the necessity of choice. Moreover most would feel that this to be an argued choice, even if the argument only amounts to shc ing that the decision for one or the other concept is arbitrary. shall meet the occasional writer who seems unaware that anyc has ever found the concept of bureaucracy problematical, but thi rare.[1] The procedure which is adopted in coming to a decision as which concept to prefer may conveniently be called a concept strategy.

There is a wide variety of such strategies. It is possible to gatl a range of definitions of bureaucracy and then attempt to find so common factor in them. An effort may be made to find some ki of majority opinion. The writer may seek to consider the obje (*denotata*) to which the term has been applied and then offer a n definition. Various criteria may be advanced to justify the adopti of an existing definition, e.g. compatibility with colloquial spee or use by an authoritative figure, or place in an influential theo A case may be made out for offering a new definition of the write own simply in the interests of clarity. A definition may be chos which facilitates measurement and field work.

Each of these strategies is represented in the discussion of t concept of bureaucracy, and attention will be drawn to them in t following pages.[2] But these strategies stem, not from the traditi of writing about bureaucracy, but from a writer's general positi on the methodology of social science. They cannot, therefore, used to organize the material of this chapter without blurring t continuities of writing which it has been the task of this book document. To preserve this developmental perspective mode writing on bureaucracy will be reviewed by taking in turn the co cepts with which we are already familiar, referring to the vario disciplinary affiliations, theoretical inclinations and conceptu strategies of the authors only when this will be of assistance explaining any deviations from, or elaborations of, the establish meanings of bureaucracy.

But before beginning that task we should briefly notice one co ceptual strategy which simply involves accepting as authoritati the concept of bureaucracy which Max Weber formulated. Such a approach clearly recommends itself to writers of textbooks, but has also been employed in more notable publications such a uzelis's *Organization and Bureaucracy* and Nettl's *Political bilization.*[3] At first sight no other method might appear to pre- e a concept so well and permit research to proceed with less ile conceptual discussion. But of course this is to neglect the iculties which subsequent commentators have found in inter- ting Weber's concept and to leave us unenlightened as to which he many interpretations is being accepted. Thus we are norm- left to assume that it is the ideal type which is being adopted not Weber's more general concept.[4] When an interpretation of ber's concept is offered, then it will normally fall within one of major categories we shall now consider.[5]

1/ Bureaucracy as rational organization

We have seen that the most difficult problem commentators Max Weber have found has been to understand the relation ween his idea of rationality and the specific characteristics he ibuted to the ideal type of bureaucracy. It has become custom- to argue that there is no necessary relationship between these racteristics and rationality, and from this the inference has been wn that there are two alternative ways of conceptualizing bur- cracy. (We have also shown that this problem has largely been he commentators' own making, but this is immaterial in this text.)

The most eloquent exponent of this point of view has been er Blau. 'Weber conceived of bureaucracy as a social mechanism t maximizes efficiency and also as a form of social organization h specific characteristics. Both these criteria cannot be part of definition, since the relationship between the attributes of a ial institution and its consequences is a question for empirical ification and not a matter of definition.'[6] Having identified these rnatives Blau has oscillated between them in his own work. In *reaucracy in Modern Society* (1956), he suggests that it might be ferable to define bureaucracy as 'organization that maximizes ciency in administration'.[7] But in the book he co-authored with Richard Scott, *Formal Organizations* (1963), he considers that term 'is used neutrally to refer to the administrative aspects of ganizations'.[8]

Other sociologists have been less prone to doubt. Francis and one state that technically 'the term bureaucracy refers to that de of organizing which is peculiarly well adapted to maintaining

stability and efficiency in organizations that are large and comple
The fact that this concept appears to have the authority of Web
name behind it has meant that it has acquired increasing popula
in the last decade. As a typical example we may cite Peter Leonar
definition: 'It simply refers to the rational and clearly defi
arrangement of activities which are directed towards fulfilling
purposes of the organization.'[10] The consequence has been a si
ation which it would be hard to parallel for apparent pervers
The sociologist is forced to admit that his idea of bureaucrac
diametrically opposed to the popular concept of bureaucracy
administrative inefficiency. As a justification he normally point
the value-laden aspect of the popular idea, his own concept be
purely 'technical' or 'neutral'.[11] The reader is left to infer t
somehow judgements on inefficiency are evaluative while those
efficiency are value-free.

It is not surprising that this concept of bureaucracy, altho
developed by sociologists, has appealed to management theor
since the idea of efficiency has been central to much of their w
ing.[12] But this observation immediately highlights the nature of t
concept. Herbert Simon has stressed the heuristic and normat
use of the idea of rationality and has pointed out that it is not p
sible to stipulate any determinate procedures which invaria
realize the ideal of organizational efficiency. This does not o
mean that research into rational organization in different socie
is bound to find many organizational forms.[13] To claim to establ
what is rational in any situation is to purport to arbitrate on
principles which the participants in that situation are applying
means very often the erection of new principles to replace those
observer discerns. Thus Blau's *Dynamics of Bureaucracy* propo
to revise the concept of rational administration and advocates c
tain practices which will ensure 'the stable attainment of organi
tional objectives'.[14] Paradoxically, the assertion of the relativity
standards of rationality is only the prelude to offering a m
universally applicable set.

The point at issue here is an illustration of what is involved
any sociological definition of an institution which has its own co
of rules. The sociologist of law, for instance, does not claim
elaborate or adjudicate on legal principles. He does not attempt
define law as 'that which accords with the principles of justice', b
rather adopts an outsider's position and studies those situatio

re men have applied rules which they call law. This position is n also to the sociologist of organizations.[15] There is a major inction to be drawn between defining bureaucracy as 'rational anization' and as 'organization where men apply criteria of onality to their action'. The latter corresponds much more ely with the spirit of Weber's ideal type. But it is a distinction ch is not normally made, and until it is this concept of bureau-cy must be seen as belonging to the same logical category as the cept which has so frequently been spurned as 'popular', anizational inefficiency.[16]

2/ Bureaucracy as organizational inefficiency

We saw how, in the nineteenth century, it was customary to ment on the pejorative overtones which the term bureaucracy in everyday language. The concept of bureaucracy as rational anization has always been the property of an academic élite, we can trace this idea back to the German administrative orists of the nineteenth century entirely through academic lications. But the concept of bureaucracy as inefficient organi-on has needed no scholarly tradition to sustain it. Moreover, se scholars who favour this concept have tended to justify it by rence to popular usage rather than by seeking academic author-At least this is so where the idea of inefficiency does not extend omprising the arrogation of power by officials, a concept with whole tradition of political theory behind it and which will be sidered later in this chapter.

The result is that this concept of organizational inefficiency kes frequent but isolated appearances in the literature of social nce. Among management theorists Marshall Dimock in par-ular has used the concept of bureaucracy as the antithesis of ninistrative vitality and managerial creativity. It is defined as e composite institutional manifestations which tend towards lexibility and depersonalisation'.[17] He attributes its growth to a le variety of factors including organizational size, the prolifera-n of rules, group introversion, and too great an emphasis on age l security. Among writers on politics a concept similar to that of mock's, though independently developed, is held by E. Strauss. *The Ruling Servants* (1961), he reserves the term bureaucracy 'the many imperfections in the structure and functioning of big ganizations'.[18] Symptoms of bureaucracy include over-devotion to precedent, lack of initiative, procrastination, proliferatior forms, duplication of effort and departmentalism.

While there may be at most a broken intellectual traditior justify labelling organizational inefficiency as bureaucracy, it i course true that writers on bureaucracy and rationality have p vided a theoretical framework for discussing inefficiency. Chapt discussed how many commentators on Weber, among wh Merton is the most notable, have shown how informal and un ticipated processes, generated by ostensibly rational organizati may occasion administrative delay and public complaints of tape. For many writers this has meant jettisoning the concept bureaucracy as rational organization, and inceed discarding implicit normative orientation involved in the concept of ratio lity. But a recent French representative of this largely Ameri tradition of writing, Michel Crozier, has crossed to the oppos side and, like Dimock and Strauss, sees bureaucracy as essentia inefficient organization.

In *The Bureaucratic Phenomenon* (1964), Crozier sees bureaucra as 'an organization that cannot correct its behavior by learni from its errors'.[19] He shows how the rules of an organization m be used by the individuals within it to their own advantage, a how, in consequence, the interest which various strata have in p serving the status quo produces rigidity of structure. Such system, Crozier argues, is badly adapted to the needs of mode business and technology. But the moment this is said the norm tive orientation of this concept of bureaucracy is apparent. T fact that Crozier and Blau contradict each other on the usage of t term bureaucracy cannot hide their commitment to very simil concepts of organizational rationality. Each places a high value flexibility and adaptability.[20]

Whether this commitment is regrettable or laudable is, in th context, beside the point. But it is striking how much Crozie analysis reflects his own dissatisfaction with French organization structure rather than registers the complaints of the participants the situation. Indeed, he acknowledges that they derive multip satisfactions from it. As with the previous concept, clarity woul be enhanced by distinguishing between inefficiency as discerned b the analyst in applying his own criteria and the situation whic arouses complaints of bureaucracy among a public. It is wort noting that this distinction is provided for in the German literatu employing both the term *Bürokratismus* and *Bürokratie*. The ner usually refers to an ethos of officialdom which antagonizes public.[21]

3/ Bureaucracy as rule by officials

The problem of normative orientation, inherent in the two viously considered concepts, is of course at the forefront again en we turn to what can claim to be the original concept of eaucracy: rule by officials. It was in this sense that de Gournay Mill used the term, and we have seen how this was a deliberate oration of the classical framework of thought about types of ernment. But, in spite of this origin in traditional political ory, this concept has been markedly less subject to the amalnation of positive and normative standpoints than the concepts have just discussed.

This ought not to be too surprising. The Greek concepts origied as much in the desire to classify as to criticize, and to a large ent it is the modern treatment of one particular concept of the ssical framework—democracy—which has led to a widespread umption that it is ill-adapted to social scientific requirements. It he modern wish to view democracy not in terms of the rule of a ss but as rule for the good of the whole people, and here clearly normative argument begins. It means that, whatever the disution of power (and it is always unevenly distributed), efforts l be made to show that true democracy exists. Hence bureaucy may be shown to be compatible with, or even necessary to, nocracy, and this issue has loomed so large that the next chapter l be devoted to it. But if the question being asked is simply 'Who power?' rather than 'Whom does power benefit?' then the conts of bureaucracy, monarchy or aristocracy can be seen as cifications of the nature of the group or individual who at any e holds power.

In spite of its relative antiquity, the line of thought which has intained the idea of bureaucracy as the rule of officials has been remely tenuous. This is partly due to the overwhelming amount attention which has been paid to the idea of bureaucracy as ional organization. But it is also attributable to the unfashionle nature of comprehensive schemes of classification in Western litical thought: such a degree of systematization is normally emed to be characteristic of Marxism and deterministic thinking in general. (We have examined in detail why the notion of offic as a ruling group has been anathema to Marxists, at least until heresies of Rizzi and Djilas.)

However, between the two world wars, there was a suffici number of notable thinkers to maintain the original concept bureaucracy. An influential definition was that of Harold Lask the *Encyclopaedia of the Social Sciences* (1930): 'Bureaucracy is term usually applied to a system of government the control which is so completely in the hands of officials that their po jeopardises the liberties of ordinary citizens.'[22] In common with nineteenth-century predecessors Laski then went on to sugg ways in which bureaucracy could be prevented. Herman Finer li wise continued the earlier practice of comparing the continent Europe with England and finding bureaucracy in the former o He insisted that bureaucracy meant government by officials.[23] distinguished student of the French civil service, W. R. Sha determined to call bureaucracy 'the exercise of power by prof sional administrators' although with that he associated the idea excessive formalism.[24] In 1937 a Belgian scholar, Daniel Warno reviewed competing concepts of bureaucracy and concluded t the increasing influence of officials was a phenomenon of suffici sociological importance that the term bureaucracy should reserved for it alone.[25]

But these definitional exercises were merely holding operatio as far as the idea of power of officials was concerned. No atten was made to develop this concept in the context of research i the other types of power which it implied. However it is also i portant to point out that even if this concept implied a multiplic of types of rule, and indeed the proponents were all committed a type other than bureaucracy, none the less the most influent theory in existence about the power of officials, Michels's 'iron l of oligarchy', denied the reality of this multiplicity. It was precis this kind of deterministic theory which inhibited the use o general classificatory scheme of governments in research. The cent development of this concept of bureaucracy has theref depended on modifying the absoluteness of the Michels's theo There has had to be a general recognition, firstly, that the issue not whether officials have power or not, but to what extent th have power; secondly, and consequently, that a typology of gover ment will be based on the *relative* power of different groups and be possible for some societies to be more bureaucratic than ers.

'he work of Arnold Brecht can be cited as an example of the mpt to do justice to the idea of a range of intensity of bureau- ic power. In his essay "How Bureaucracies Develop and Func- " (1954), he defines bureaucracy as 'government by officials' and inguishes two senses of power: the legal right to give orders, and power to get something done.[26] Officials may possess either e of power, either wholly or partially, and wherever there are cials they will possess some amount of the one or the other type, Brecht illustrates this thesis to show that there are no countries hout bureaucracy. Karl Wittfogel's classic work, *Oriental potism* (1957), is the best example of research into the extreme e of bureaucratic power in total form. He develops what he con- ers to be the suppressed implications of Marx's concept of an atic type of society and argues that the class structure of histori- empires such as China was based essentially on the relations of n to the state apparatus. At the heart of this apparatus were the cials.

Credit for the nearest approach to elaborating the full typology rule which this concept of bureaucracy implies must go to rold Lasswell and Abraham Kaplan. In *Power and Society* 50), they outline eight forms of rule, classified according to the ss from which the rulers are recruited: bureaucracy ('the form of e in which the élite is composed of officials'), aristocracy, etho- cy, democracy, virocracy, plutocracy, technocracy and ideo- cy.[27] Although the empirical basis of this 'framework for poli- al enquiry' is merely sketched, and it has not been systematically plied, it does suggest the appropriate context for the develop- nt of this concept of bureaucracy as rule by officials. A recent empt to analyse one of those forms of rule (though without erence to Lasswell) is Jean Meynaud's *Technocracy* (1968). It ovides some validation of at least part of the Lasswell-Kaplan mework in that Meynaud's examination of power stemming m technical expertise involves him in discussing the power that ues from a predetermined role in an institutional system, i.e. reaucracy.[28]

We have stressed the use of this concept of bureaucracy as part an analytical framework for the study of power. At the same time has been made clear that the linking of this idea of bureaucracy with the theory that all administrative officials acquire po means that any system of public administration can be seen exemplify bureaucracy. But such a view of public administrat may appear distinctly blinkered, for the functions of public admi tration within society are far more manifold than merely provid members of a governing élite. Therefore public administration often been referred to as bureaucracy without any special refere to the possession of power being implied. It is to this apparen unimpeachably neutral concept that we now turn.

4/ Bureaucracy as public administration

Paradoxically the most influential proponent of this see ingly neutral concept of bureaucracy was Mussolini. We have s how well such a concept fitted into the Fascists' programme absorbing society into the state and how closely related it was Michels's desire for a neutral concept to play a part in a scient theory of power. Of course Michels's theory led to viewing burea cracy as an element of any organizational structure, and we sh examine this line of thought later, but for many the special nat of the state, as seen either by its conservative *laissez-faire* econon opponents or its Fascist supporters, meant reserving the term public administration.

While right-wing thinkers have found this concept of burea cracy useful it would be a mistake to infer that those who emp this concept are bound to be right wing. It is an idea to be fou widely in the most dispassionate type of political science. But it interesting that those scholars who have made a particular study Italy tend to incorporate this idea into their work.[29] Thus Tay Cole, who discussed Italy's Fascist bureaucracy in the 1930s, intr duces his *The Canadian Bureaucracy* (1949), with the followi definition: 'The term "bureaucracy" is not used here in an invi ous sense . . . but simply refers to a group of human beings or er ployees who are performing definite functions considered essent by a community.'[30] He proceeds to explain that he does not want use the term 'civil service' because of its restricted legal sense whi prevents it from covering the full range of public employees.

This conceptualization requires two comments. It should fir be noted how major emphasis is placed upon the association aspect of bureaucracy, i.e. on the group performing functio rather than on the functions themselves. With every concept eaucracy, as was pointed out in the first chapter, there is an ytical tendency to stress either the group or the activity, to k primarily in institutional or associational terms.[31] The second ment is that, although the functions this group performs are nite', they are left undefined, and, although they are 'con- red essential', it is not clear who is doing the considering. If we nine this second point more closely we shall find a partial lanation for the emphasis on bureaucracy as a group of eaucrats.

'here is great diversity in the kinds of activities which are under- n by public employees in any one society and there are large erences between societies as to the functions the state assumes. theory of public administration can account for the fact that ool teachers are civil servants in one country and not another. If lic administration is considered to comprise the tasks which lic employees have, then the conceptual focus is not provided the nature of the tasks but by the fact that a number of indivi- ls share a characteristic which gives them a common interest, employment by the state. For comparative purposes this is the st obvious constant feature.

ven if we attempt to abstract from the general activities of state ployees an area we call 'pure' administration we find no struc- al feature to distinguish civil services from organizations in eral, a point which our next concept of bureaucracy accom- dates. If there is a crucial differentiating characteristic of civil vices it is their use of a vague criterion in decision making known 'the public interest'. The difficulties in operating this criterion notorious. Its definition is a matter of political conflict, and refore theoretically out of the hands of civil servants, but any inition is so dependent on interpretation that there can be no ambiguous central determination of its nature. It is interpreted t is implemented, and that process is in the hands of civil serv- s: which brings us back to considering the values and attitudes of bureaucrats as a group.

The identification of bureaucracy with public administration s, in recent years, usually been a component in the attempt to ke the latter a unit of analysis in broad comparative studies or a general system approach to political life. The result has been concentrate far more on bureaucracy as a pressure group and a mative influence on societal values than upon processes of administration. These processes may be summed up in term content-less as 'A civil service is engaged in meeting the syste goals of society as a whole', or 'Bureaucratic apparatus is one of institutions through which goal gratification activity is performe The nature of the activities is elusive, but the group is cle visible.

There are many well-known comparative studies of bureauc in this sense. Morstein Marx's *The Administrative State* (19 proposes a classification of bureaucracies into four types: Guardian bureaucracy, as in traditional China or Prussia; Caste bureaucracy, dependent on recruitment from one class o the Patronage bureaucracy, as in nineteenth-century Englan under the Jacksonian system in the United States; and the M bureaucracy, tending to be middle class and characterizing mod Western societies.[33] But Morstein Marx also considers other c cepts of bureaucracy and makes use of them for analysing o aspects of public administration.

S. N. Eisenstadt's *The Political Systems of Empires* (1963), d not offer a formal definition but normally treats bureaucracy as body of administrative officials and, after the ruling élite, 'the group participating in the political struggle'.[34] This study twenty-seven historical empires outlines a classification of bure cracies according to their involvement in the political proc They might be (1) service-oriented to rulers and major so strata; (2) totally subservient to the ruler; (3) autonomous and ented to its own advantage; (4) self-oriented but also serving polity in general rather than any specific strata.

This concept has been put to considerable use in recent stu of developing societies. It is common to most of the essays in Palombara's collection, *Bureaucracy and Political Developm* (1963). J. T. Dorsey, in his essay on Vietnam, typically defi bureaucracy as 'the "public" or civil governmental administrat components of political systems'.[35] La Palombara concedes vagueness of this concept of bureaucracy when he introduces volume. On occasions he says it must be seen as encompassing public servants, but at other times only those at a high level. consequence it is 'an accordion-like conceptualization'.[36] It is the work of another contributor to this volume, Fred W. Rig that we find this concept most fully developed, and, in consequen its particular problems most fully exposed.

ı his paper "Agraria and Industria—Toward a Typology of ıparative Administration" (1957), Riggs takes on the task of sing a conceptual framework which would be capable of analys- public administration in societies as diverse as traditional China contemporary United States.[37] He finds that the idea of inistration as the implementation of policies laid down by a ılature is too limited to industrial societies and suggests a defini- of 'public administrative system' as 'structures for allocating ls and services in a government'.[38] He finds that his concept of :aucracy overlaps this, although not completely, and views it as llective term 'to refer to those whose major occupation or pro- ion is governmental work and who are recruited for this work ugh means which are neither hereditary nor elective'.[39] Such a :ept allows him to do justice to the varying degrees of power :aucracies may have, and also leaves room for other categories ersons to be involved in the tasks of administration.

ut these distinctions become difficult to maintain in the course nalysis. The connections between agrarian bureaucracies and :ocracies are close enough for recruitment to the former to be n *de facto* hereditary. The fact of office-holding remains even ıe form of recruitment is not specified. But to think of Riggs' :aucrats simply as office-holders is still too specific since the on of an office with a defined authority is more appropriate to narrow conception of administration he rejects. Perhaps for e reasons Riggs reverts to seeing administration in more tradi- al terms as 'the process by which policies are implemented' in 1964 publication, *Administration in Developing Countries*.[40] e bureaucrats seem simply to be government officials and this he concept he acknowledges in his contribution to the La mbara collection.[41]

'he 'accordion-like' nature of this concept must be recognized ough it is not by any means alone among social science con- ts in having this characteristic. In this case the problems arise be- se of the indefiniteness of the concept of public administration the immense difficulties there are in adapting it for com- ative analysis. Here the idea of bureaucracy, by directing atten- to an active political group, may be seen as clarifying issues. ıs Almond and Coleman see the bureaucracy as one interest ıp among many in *The Politics of Developing Areas* (1960). But ı the theoretical content of the concept becomes so thin that it

can easily be absorbed into such a general category as 'politici
A well-known exponent of systems analysis of politics, D
Easton, has a category, the 'authorities', into which governn
officials fit without special mention.[42] But if there is no wis
focus attention on the political pressure group but rather to fi
concept which will highlight the activity involved in public admi
tration, then one must turn to the idea of bureaucracy devel
as part of a theory of administration in any organization.

5/ Bureaucracy as administration by offic

We have seen how Max Weber's general concept of bur
cracy (as distinct from the ideal type) simply amounted to
ministration by appointed officials. But this concept was lir
with an explicit framework for organizational analysis in w
organizations were seen as tripartite structures in which admi
trative staffs exercising day to day authority were the central
Where these staffs were made up of appointees one could ta
bureaucracies. It is fair to see this concept of a specialized func
within organizations known as administration as being at the h
of Weber's theory of bureaucracy. Since his time this concept
been maintained particularly strongly by those who have n
close study of Weber. Argument among them has centred
whether modern administrative systems have general feature
addition to being staffed by appointed officials and whether
ideal type characteristics are the best summary of mo
administration.

This concept is especially prevalent in European writing,
this must be attributed to the nature of Continental administra
as much as to the influence of Weber. Karl Renner points ou
Demokratie und Bureaukratie (1947), how concerned the Euro
is with the ideas of office and hierarchy.[43] He argues that all or
izations have a bureaucratic apparatus and it is an important
that the separateness of this apparatus of officials has been r
forced by long-established methods of allocating prestige
European systems of social stratification. H. P. Bahrdt's *In*
triebürokratie (1958), is an excellent example of the use of
concept in a non-government context.[44] He examines the gro
of bureaucracy in industry and asks how far automation of o
routines will alter concepts of administrative organization.
Sultan's essay "Bürokratie und Politische Machtbildung" (19

ks at this concept against a broad background of organizations l considers that the growth of bureaucracy is simply a function he size of an organization.[45]

American scholars writing in the European tradition on this sub- also find this a congenial concept. It is employed by Reinhard ndix in *Work and Authority in Industry* (1956), although he pre- s to speak of the growth of the administrative sector as bureau- tization. We have mentioned how Peter Blau has reverted to s concept after his earlier adherence to the idea of rational anization.[46] The British historian G. E. Aylmer reviews differ- concepts of bureaucracy to find one suitable for his study of the l service of Charles I, *The King's Servants* (1961), and decides t historians will find it most useful 'to think of bureaucracy as erring to certain methods of administration'.[47] As examples of se methods he mentions professionalism, regular hierarchy, ision into departments and heavy reliance on written records. this sense, he says, England can be said to have had a bureau- cy since the twelfth century.

The American political scientist, Wallace Sayre, compiled a ilar list of characteristics of the administration of any large com- x organization: specialization of tasks, hierarchy of authority, ly of rules, system of records and personnel with specialized ls and roles.[48] Such a list is not dissimilar to Weber's, but it is cial that no comment is made as to any level of rationality. Yet ould be wrong to suppose that the universality of these features non-controversial. We have already mentioned A. L. Stinch- nbe's suggestion that the building industry provides a good mple of non-centralized administration where control is rcised by independent professional bodies.[49]

Carl Friedrich's efforts to establish the common features of dern administrative systems were also mentioned in the context liscussing his criticisms of Weber.[50] The conceptual strategy he ocates as an alternative to Weber's ideal type method—the tematic comparison of those phenomena known as bureaucra- s—has become extremely influential. But if we consider that ategy and Friedrich's general thinking about bureaucracy we will l that it tends to veer away from considering features of adminis- ion and towards a more comprehensive concept of organization. 1932, in collaboration with T. Cole, he wrote *Responsible reaucracy—A study of the Swiss Civil Service*. He makes the point there that bureaucracy is to be found as much outside inside government. As we have already implied, such a percepti is a necessary precondition for developing a concept appropri for all kinds of administration. But he makes the further point t administration and policy are normally too sharply distinguish and it is quite usual to find agencies which combine these functio So the structural and behavioural elements which for Friedr make up bureaucracy are found in a wide variety of organizatio and they comprise more than mere administration. But if centr zation, differentiation of functions or qualification for office c characterize policy-making agencies as well as administration, c they not also be features of that which is administered? Then i the organization as a whole which is the subject of analysis. T concept of bureaucracy is on the verge of being recast once aga

6/ Bureaucracy as the organization

Weber's trichotomous view of organizations correspond well with the hierarchic images of society of his own time. Yet was prepared to admit, even to emphasize, that the administra gained power to determine policy. At the same time his idea of priest and officer being transformed into bureaucrats, while il minating, stopped short of viewing administrative functions diffused throughout an organizational hierarchy. For Weber a ministration meant the exercise of authority. There had to be so who only received and never gave orders. Yet the mode of organ ing the administrative staff which he called the ideal type bureaucracy involved no principles which could not be applied the structuring of the whole membership of an organization. T requirements of professional qualification, full-time commitme strict separation of the individual's resources from those of his j contractual employment, etc., can be attached to any organizatio position. If these principles were applied generally and at the sa time the fact of diffuse distribution of authority throughout organization was recognized, it would not be inappropriate to sp of the whole structure as a bureaucracy. From being a sub-syst bureaucracy would become the system in its entirety.

It is not possible to impute this line of argument directly a wholly to any one author. But it does briefly indicate how it happened that Weber has been taken as a starting point, only the position to be reached that organization and bureaucracy garded as synonymous. The very fact of change in organizational ucture since his time has meant the adaptation and extension of s terminology. We shall return to this issue in the concluding apter but for the moment we may note an important indicator of anging social reality: in popular parlance it is common now to k of any large organization as a bureaucracy. While it would be fficult to confirm this with any degree of certainty, it is likely that is kind of statement: 'The college, from the standpoint of social alysis, is simply one bureaucracy among many others', would ve sounded quite foreign to nineteenth-century ears,[51] whereas no longer seems strange to speak of schools, armies, churches and spitals as bureaucracies.

In general, therefore, those modern social scientists who write organizations as bureaucracies do not rely on a complex modi- ation of Weber's theory to justify their concept. They can use eryday language as their authority. Talcott Parsons, introducing s collection of essays, *Structure and Process in Modern Societies* 960), says: 'One of the most salient structural characteristics of ch a society is the prominence in it of relatively large-scale ganisations with specialised functions, what rather loosely tend be called "bureaucracies" '.[52] Others are less guarded about the opriety of this usage. We may cite Hyneman: 'bureaucracy as an straction is big organisation, and any big organisation is speci- ally a bureaucracy'; Simon that bureaucracy is 'an approximate nonym for large scale organisation'; Presthus, 'the terms "big ganisation" and "bureaucratic structures" are synonymous'; and tzioni, 'There are many synonyms for the term, *organisation*. One, *reaucracy*, has two disadvantages.'[53]

The disadvantages Etzioni has in mind are the popular negative nnotations and the possible assumption by those familiar with Max Weber's work that the organization would be ordered along e lines of the ideal type. This second possibility has concerned hers too. Just as Friedrich advocates the comparative study of stems of administration, so those who have identified bureaucracy ith the organization as a whole have supported research to estab- sh what dimensions do characterize organizations. Of course such programme is itself dependent on the concept of organization hich is held at the outset of research. Some think of organizations nly as social units oriented to specific goals. Others implicitly or xplicitly have a wide concept of organization and limit their field of research to complex, or large-scale, or formal, or modern org nizations. Then, as Ferrel Heady writes, 'bureaucracy is a form organization. Organizations either are bureaucracies or they a not, depending on whether or not they have these characteristics.'

There are almost as many listings of the characteristics maki up bureaucracy as there are authors who hold this concept. Pres hus lists size, specialization, hierarchy, status authority, oligarch co-optation, rationality and 'efficiency'; Bennis mentions a cha of command, rules, division of labour, selection on ground individual competence and impersonality; Heady reduces the li to three items for which he claims there is 'substantial' agreemen hierarchy, differentiation or specialization, and qualification competence.[55] The fact that Heady introduces the notion of 'sul stantial agreement' between authors suggests another conceptu strategy which is becoming fashionable among the proponents this concept. With the proliferation of different lists of characteri tics it is now possible to undertake an 'empirical' research proje to determine what is common to the lists. A new depiction of bu eaucracy results, which includes those characteristics on whic there is general agreement.[56] But the search for such a consensu may result in such a diversity of items being revealed that in the en doubt is cast upon the usefulness of the concept of bureaucracy. It may appear as more of an impediment than an aid to agreed co ceptual framework for the comparative study of organizations.

Bureaucracy as organization is also a difficult idea. The facts organizational structure are not unambiguous data, to be recorde by anyone who might care to observe, but abstract and elusiv phenomena which depend on interpretative inventiveness. In pa ticular, the boundaries of organizations are difficult to draw. Ju as it proved complicated to draw a line between administration an organization, so it is hard to see where organization ends an society begins. Hierarchy, rules, division of labour, careers, qual fications seem to pervade modern society, and are not simpl housed in separate organizations. Perhaps we can speak of organi zations as being bureaucratic only because they are a part of wider bureaucracy—modern society itself.

7/ Bureaucracy as modern society

We cannot be surprised by what may be called the apothe osis of bureaucracy, its acceptance into that pantheon of idea hich attempt to capture the essence of a society and among which e such concepts as democracy, communism, capitalism and socism. It may be seen as a development inherent in an idea which in conception was set on the same plane as democracy, aristocracy d monarchy. It is just as appropriate to employ 'democratic' as epithet for a society as for a government. But if this development has always been a potentiality, we should not underestimate e arduousness of the gestation period.

The tradition of Western thought about societal types was gely captured by Marx and his followers. We have already exained why the concept of bureaucracy could not occupy a dominnt place in Marxist thought. The idea of a bureaucratic society uld only be developed by Marxist heretics. Rizzi and Djilas ovide examples. Among the opponents of Marxism the most table approximation to the idea of society as bureaucracy is in osca's work. Since Mosca, the most widely known Western exession of the view that society is dominated by bureaucrats is at made in James Burnham in 1941: *The Managerial Revolution* gnificantly enough, the author was formerly a Marxist). While essing the importance of the managerial group in the economy, rnham argues in that book that there is no sharp separation tween them and political officials. 'To say that the ruling class is e managers is almost the same thing as to say that it is the state reaucracy.'[58]

However, even if Burnham envisages the fusion of state and ivate management, it is none the less true that his theory, like at of Marx or of Mosca, considers a society's type to be stamped it by the character of its ruling class. Mosca and Burnham are king of bureaucratic societies largely in the sense of societies led by bureaucracies rather than societies which have become reaucracies. The difference between the two concepts is wide. rl Wittfogel, for instance, speaks of bureaucratic society where undifferentiated peasantry making up perhaps 95 per cent of the pulation supports the ruling bureaucratic class. The societies ich Djilas analyses have highly differentiated proletariats in ich every member has a specified organizational role; the whole ucture may be seen as bureaucracy.

The ideological desire for the fusion of state and society became ost concrete in Italian Fascism. But commentators on Fascist ly have seen the corporate state as a framework fitted over an order which was well adapted to it.[59] Karl Mannheim has argu that changes in social structure in the twentieth century have in a case made the opposition of the concepts of state and society out date. 'This dualism usually equates "state" with "bureaucrac and society with the conglomeration of vigorous organisations t successfully claim the epithets "free and private" '.[60] He finds t this dualism is obsolete for several reasons. In respect of pow methods of recruitment, public significance and the personal types of members, he sees no difference between private and pub organizations. Their spheres overlap so that 'public responsibil is interwoven in the whole fabric of society'.[61]

A similar conclusion has been reached by those who have beg their analysis at the other end and considered the internal struct of organizations. As we have shown in the context of argument w Weber it has become normal to stress that the framework of orga izational regulations reflects wider social structure. Even th areas of social life which seem to be interstitial, and outside the s control of any one organization, exhibit codes of rules which m have emerged out of a common interest in formalizing relatio for example in areas as different as business and sport. We can Crozier's emphasis on the bureaucratic culture of France as a c mination of this way of thinking.[62] As R. V. Presthus has express this in *The Organizational Society* (1962), 'organizations are inde miniatures of society'. Since he regards 'big organizations' a 'bureaucratic structures' as synonymous we can conclude that i not incongruous to think of bureaucracy as a type of society.[63]

It is interesting to see how this culminating point has also be implied in the use of the idea of bureaucratization. Very often t term has been used simply to connote the growth of bureaucra Therefore it may take on as many meanings as bureaucracy its But it is a verbal substantive. It implies a unit, be it group society, which is being bureaucratized. In the 1920s it was qu normal to speak of the bureaucratization of the firm, meaning introduction of systematic administration and the growth of number of purely administrative employees.[64] But the impact this process is not limited to the firm. Its employees are also me bers of society and take to it their organizational experience. As firm grows its influence as a unit increases. If the firm itsel viewed as a bureaucracy then we can conceive of the bureaucrati tion of society in terms of an increase in the number and size of

nizations. But we can also see bureaucratization as the sub-
ion of society to the influence of the attitudes and values of
eaucrats, or, in Arnold Gehlen's words, 'the development of an
nanent perfectionism'.[65]
. N. Eisenstadt draws a distinction between the growth of bur-
cracy and bureaucratization which he defines as the 'excessive
ination by the bureaucracy of parts of its environment'.[66] But
ever expanding nature of the concept of bureaucracy means that
ractice this distinction must break down. For the growth of
eaucracies (administrations or organizations) proceeds by the
inual incorporation of new elements into the bureaucracy, so
they become constituent parts of it.[67] The growth of organi-
ons involves the bureaucratization of society, and that is
amount to society becoming bureaucracy.

What we have outlined here is complex. It requires further
rpretation and we shall return to that task. But, before that, it
orth taking a brief look at the various remedies which have been
cribed for bureaucracy. Those who advocate alternatives, by
lication specify all the more clearly the nature of the condition
seek to remedy.

6/Bureaucracy and the Theorists of Democracy

The changing intellectual context

The idea of bureaucracy arose out of a concern for proper place of the official in modern government. We have se in particular, how the nineteenth-century writers contrasted b eaucracy with democracy. They discerned numerous ways which the use and usages of public officials subverted democr values. In other words, the phenomena which were held to con tute bureaucracy were defined as significant topics for analysis their relation to the values of democracy, and, because of th conflict with those values, were held to be problems requiring so tion. Similarly, the remedies which were suggested for bureaucr were designed to realize the very values which defined the nat of the disease. It follows that as the values of democracy w reformulated so the concept of bureaucracy was recast.

When the evaluative elements in the nineteenth-century the of bureaucracy are exposed so clearly, an easy explanation of neglect of that literature suggests itself. Much effort has been sp in this century in separating the advocacy of values from the an sis of facts. Our discussions have reflected this. We have analy ideological literature separately from modern social science. It m well appear that the old argument about the relation of democr and bureaucracy has been rendered futile by the demonstrat that it involves two sets of problems: the specification of the val of democracy, and the gathering of data about the place of pu officials in modern government.

Yet the problem of bureaucracy is still raised. Scholars citizens are still concerned to offer solutions in the light of th conception of true democracy. We can still find conceptualizati of bureaucracy which would have fitted easily into nineteen century discussions. For example, Herman Finer, reviewing so of the more indiscriminate accusations of bureaucracy made in 1940s, considers that charge appropriate only where there is ministration by bureaus of government officials who are abus

function for which they were appointed'.[1] The dual character
his concept, both empirical and normative, should be apparent.
demonstrate the existence of bureaucracy it is not sufficient
ply to indicate the mode of behaviour of public officials. It
t be shown that this behaviour does not correspond with their
, 'the function for which they were appointed'. But this func-
is always in dispute. It is the subject of the endless debate
ut the true nature of democracy.

Ve are concerned in this chapter with those who still pose 'the
blem of bureaucracy' and suggest solutions to it. So long as
e are types of public officials and sets of values which are held
e an inherent part of 'real' democracy this 'problem of bureau-
y' will continue to be raised. Moreover, it would be quite mis-
n to suppose that modern advances in social and political
nce have rendered the old problem settings redundant and no
ger important. On the contrary, discussion has been raised to
levels of sophistication and of importance. We should recall
Max Weber was one of the major advocates of the clear separa-
of factual statements from evaluative judgements. Yet he did
retreat from suggesting answers to the problem of the relation-
of bureaucracy to democracy. He analysed this issue with
racteristic dispassion. He drew the line so clearly between the
modes of discourse only to mark the point when he was
nging from the one to the other.[2]

'he writing which followed may be seen as occupying a position
ewhere between ideology and social science. It is not ideological
he sense of directly advocating certain values. Rather it seeks to
lyse values for their meaning and implications. Indeed the per-
al commitment of the analyst to those values is not required. It
ot 'social scientific' in the sense of having as a prime purpose the
mulation of propositions of a general and explanatory nature
ut how institutions operate. Instead, it sifts the propositions of
al science to discover information which is *significant* for cer-
value positions. But clearly it is a literature which is dependent
he prior separation of fact and value, and many would see it as
racteristic of Western political thought. We shall not argue
ut its proper designation—whether it should be labelled politi-
theory, philosophy or science. It is sufficient, in this context, to
its exponents 'the theorists of democracy'.

t cannot be denied that it is often very difficult to determine what is ideological and what is social scientific, and, since the def tion of this intermediate category is dependent on such a disti tion, we must be prepared to find ambiguously located writi We have already discovered that much of what is written aro the concepts of bureaucracy as rational or inefficient adminis tion involves the application of evaluative criteria and the sp fication of the nature of those values. It was the intention rat than the achievement of those writers which warranted discus those concepts in the previous chapter and not in this. Similarly can turn to East European discussions of the way to realize pop sovereignty through local self-government and find that this longs properly to the literature of the theorists of democra Certainly we shall have to consider, after discussing their w whether the democratic theorists do not, after all, allow unexamined ideology to colour their reasoning.

If the above analysis is correct the concept of bureaucracy we discussing here cannot be equated with any of the concepts of previous chapter, although any of those may at one time or ano be considered as an aspect of the threat to democracy. Even concept of bureaucracy as rule by officials, while closest to ni teenth-century preoccupations, has been incorporated into neu typologies of government and is regarded as permitting argun as to whether it is or is not compatible with the idea of democra It must be made quite clear at the outset of this discussion that concept under scrutiny is of public officials defeating the object democracy. It differs, therefore, from the concepts considere the previous chapter in its high evaluative content and the co quent relativity of its application to empirical phenomena. Whe the operations of public officials are to be judged as bureauc depends on how the values of democracy are construed and w of them are held to be offended. For each interpretation of de cracy there is a corresponding idea of bureaucracy.

At this point a tiresome, but unavoidable, terminological is must be raised. Not every writer on the theme of the threa democracy from officialdom calls that threat 'bureaucracy'. M do, but the majority reserve the term for one or other of the c cepts discussed in the previous chapter. Sometimes this differe in usage may be symptomatic of deeper disagreements. Friedri use of the term for administration by officials signifies his b that it is not the power of officials which presents a problem, way in which that power is used. Herman Finer's reservation ureaucracy' for the situation where officials threaten demo- y expresses his disagreement with that position. But both drich and Finer are concerned with the problem of the com- bility of the practices of modern public administration with the es of democracy. In the ensuing pages we shall call this 'the lem of bureaucracy'. This phrase is conveniently ambiguous r as terminology is concerned. It does not make clear whether problem is *called* bureaucracy, as with Finer, or is *posed by* aucracy, as with Friedrich. What concerns us primarily is not varying terminology, but the identity of the concept.

e may view the increasing sophistication of argument about problem of bureaucracy by the theorists of democracy simply facet of intellectual development, the result of the refinement hilosophical analysis and the accumulation of scientific evi- ce. But it can also be seen as a response to new factors in the al environment. Put at its simplest level, the application of the of democracy to a city state and to an industrialized society a population of 50 million is bound to give different results. ce, while we can point to certain basic principles which would eld to inhere in democracy in both the eighteenth and twentieth uries—that government must express the will of the governed, popularly elected representatives should have a major share of rnment, that the rule of law must regulate governmental pro- ure, that the governed should be informed of the decisions n on their behalf—the very fact of the growth of huge cadres of lic officials raises problem to which those principles give no ct answers.

he bulk of constitutional theory in the nineteenth century was oted to elaborating the division of functions between legislative, utive and judicial organs of the democratic state. Minimal ntion was given to specifying the place of the public official in scheme. His purely instrumental position was largely assumed. as administration has loomed larger and larger, to become rded as the core of modern government, the criterion of instru- tality has increasingly been seen as an inadequate means for ifying the nature of democratic administration. Different eria, such as accountability, responsibility, responsiveness, or esentativeness, are held to be the appropriate standards implied he values of democracy, to which public services must be kept if they are not to become bureaucracies. We shall see how eac these criteria is used in attempts both to diagnose and to cure problem of bureaucracy, and we shall see that each involve different interpretation of what is most basic to the concep democracy.

The diagnosis of bureaucracy

We may distinguish three basic positions as to the functi of public officials in the democratic state. The first is that offic have acquired too much power and need to be brought bac their proper functions. The second is that officials necessarily h ever growing power and the task is to see that this is exerci wisely. The third is that power necessarily accrues to officials the quest should be for methods whereby their services migh dispensed with altogether.

Of these positions, the third is clearly the most radical but the least clearly articulated; the second the most orthodox, and first is nearest to the concerns of the nineteenth century. It been most popular with lawyers, for reasons which will rapidl apparent. The threat to democracy is not seen as arising from incompetence of public officials, but almost from their exces reliability and diligence. The most celebrated exposition of theme is that of Lord Chief Justice Hewart in *The New Despo* (1929). The root of the problem he sees as the increasing amo of delegated legislation and power to adjudicate which belong the modern civil service. Statutes are passed which allow detail be filled in subsequently by officials, provision is made for dep mental regulations to have the force of law, decisions are m against which the citizen has no recourse at law. He sees such p tices emerging from an ethos which regards the permanent offi as the expert and representative government as a hindrance efficient transaction of public business.

Hewart's book caused sufficient alarm in Britain for a Commi on Ministers' Powers to be set up. Its report in 1932 concluded t delegated legislation was an inevitable feature of modern gove ment. It allowed Parliament to concentrate on basic principles ensured that these were operated with flexibility.[5] In the Uni States an equivalent to Hewart's treatise is J. M. Beck's *Wonderland of Bureaucracy* (1932), which bears the sub-title, study of the growth of bureaucracy in the federal government

destructive effect upon the constitution'. Beck, a former solicitor
neral, draws on Hewart but extends his analysis to a broader
itical front and attacks the growth of a socialistic state. He takes
stand on what he calls the great objectives of the Constitutional
nvention and especially on article 1, section 8 of the Constitu-
n which provides for taxes to be collected 'for the general welfare
the United States'. He argues that this phrase was meant to im-
se limits on government but that it has been construed so as to
e almost unlimited powers.[6] Under the protection of this article,
administration drafts extensive legislation, and puts itself in
position of prosecutor, jury and judge.

This theme has been taken up repeatedly since the 1930s and
been particularly popular with opponents of socialism.[7] Among
fessional students of government, however, it has taken a modi-
l form. The tendency is to argue that delegated legislation is here
stay. The problem is that it has tended to outstrip the standard
thods of direction and control which have been used in the past.
iters such as Herman Finer and C. S. Hyneman do not dis-
ard the danger to democracy in the modern development of
blic administration, but they tend to see it as potential rather
n actual. The appropriate criterion against which to measure
nocratic public administration is the responsibility of officials,
the sense of arrangements existing which ensure that their
ions will be scrutinized, corrected or punished as need be.[8]
here such arrangements break down the problem of bureaucracy
ses.

When we turn to the second of the positions on the functions of
public officials which we have distinguished, we find that
er's and Hyneman's views are one side of an important argu-
nt in the modern study of government. While they agree that
official is more involved than ever in complex policy-forming
ks, their emphasis is on the formal limits within which this task
y be executed. C. J. Friedrich's name is particularly associated
h the view that the formal delimitation of the scope of official
ivity is less important for democracy than the type of advice
ich the official gives and the spirit in which he interprets his
ks. The policy-making role of the official is not something to be
dgingly conceded, but is a vital aspect of his tasks. He sees the
tinction of policy making and execution as overdrawn.[9] Some
those who follow this line of argument extend it to the point of

offering a redefinition of public administration to include pol formulation.[10]

This different emphasis on the functions of public officials volves a different interpretation of what is to be understood democratic administration and hence a different perspective on problem of bureaucracy. Finer's elucidation of the criterion responsibility to mean accountability is replaced by a concern the responsiveness of the official to public needs. Another way expressing this contrast is through considering the differing empl sis on the concept of democracy which it involves. Those who co sider the functions of the official in danger of being over-extend are concerned primarily with the ideas of the rule of law a governmental control by elected representatives. Those who beli that the policy-making functions of officials are insufficien appreciated are more intent on developing the ideas of governm expressing a basic popular will and of a free flow of informati between governors and governed.[11]

From this standpoint the problem of bureaucracy arises wh officials fail to understand or respond to public needs. The oc sions on which this may happen vary, and, indeed, it may oc even when formal control procedures are tightly drawn. On t interpretation the German civil service was not responding to pu lic needs and was acting irresponsibly in co-operating with Hit even though they were fulfilling their legal obligations. At anot extreme, public officials who fail to obtain necessary professio expertise and fail to make use of specialized knowledge are a non-responsive. In the formulation and interpretation of policy t official is expected to make use of the best sources of informati and maintain contact with all levels of the public.[12]

This last requirement leads to an elaboration of the criterion responsiveness in the direction of representativeness. It has be argued that the free flow of information between officials a public is dependent on a shared culture, on a set of mutual und standings which can only be achieved if in fact officials are dra from all segments of a community. Responsiveness is made depend on the scope of recruitment procedures. J. D. Kingsl advances this view in his study of the British civil service, *Rep sentative Bureaucracy* (1944). He argues that the civil servant is 'permanent politician' upon whose views the policy of a modern go ernment is greatly reliant.[13] But the process of recruitment produc ervice with a narrow class background, adapted to working h Conservative Party politicians but likely to be in conflict with abour Party government. In the event, Labour Party politicians e gone out of their way to stress the dedication of their officials, the limitations of social background are often mentioned as an ect of the problem of bureaucracy in other contexts.[14] Thus Sjöberg argues that public administration is insensitive to the er class and that since that class cannot understand public ad- nistration there is bound to be conflict between that class and cials. He records how the Negro leadership has attacked the S. Department of Labor for its assumption that it is the Negro er-class family which requires restructuring rather than the ninistrative system.[15]

This emphasis on the group characteristics of civil services can d to the third point of view concerning the functions of public cials which was mentioned at the beginning of this section. On s view the very existence of a body of public officials, defined as arate from the general population even if drawn representatively m it, with its own professional standards, must lead to the forma- n of sectional interests. An identity of values between officials d the public cannot be expected and the problem of bureaucracy nherent in the situation. This radical position, which owes much Marx and sociological analyses of bureaucracy, sees the conflict ween democracy and public administration as inevitable in erentiated societies with distinct administrative staffs. Only the m of the conflict alters. It may take extreme forms, such as inter- ence by civil servants in elections or strike action calculated to vert the state. It may be expressed more mildly, such as by ance with sectional interests, resistance to outside inspection, or ply activity as any other political pressure group.[16]

At its most basic the dilemma which is posed is this: no special up in society can reflect the interests of all because it has erests of its own. This sectional interest will always be expressed olicy making while the various interests of other groups will be iably realized. Any public policy decision will be a political one which the sectional interest will be intimately bound. F. E. urke has examined the problems of secrecy and publicity as cial cases of this dilemma. Secrecy in public administration, ognized by Weber as a source of bureaucratic power, has been prevalent in the United States than in Europe. But its opposite,

publicity, can equally well serve as a means of enhancing
power of public agencies. It can be used to raise the level of pul
support in the community and in special interest groups, and i
impossible to distinguish clearly between the contribution to
public interest and the ambitions of the agency.[17]

No easy remedy seems to offer itself for this third construct
of the problem of bureaucracy, but before considering this issue
must return to the two earlier positions.

The remedies for bureaucracy

As the concept of the problem varies, so do the remed
that are proposed. Those who are concerned by the degree
involvement by officials in policy making and the range of th
discretion advocate various kinds of formal control mechanis
The particular type of control which is favoured varies accord
to the area of official power which is under scrutiny. The pul
official can exercise influence on decisions before they are made
giving advice or sifting information. The decision which is m
may formally confer wide discretionary powers on those who h
to implement it, or such powers may *de facto* come to exist beca
the decision is open to various interpretations. Furthermore, th
opportunities for the official to exercise power exist at all level
government, from relations with ministers to direct dealings w
the public, from foreign policy decisions to an individual's inco
tax assessment.

Hence the proposals which are made range from greater con
by representative bodies to more legal protection for the citize
the form of administrative law. Hewart would prefer to see the
of discretionary legislation altogether, while others look to
example of France for an elaborated system of law governing
relations of officials and citizens.[18] In Britain the idea of ministe
responsibility and the subjection of ministers to the parliamen
question have been regarded as the main form of popular cont
but, in recent years, there has been support for the idea of pa
amentary committees to investigate departmental policy on anal
with congressional committees in the United States.[19] A furt
alternative is the advocation of new formal agencies of control o
side the established representative and legal institutions. For
ample W. W. Boyer proposes an Office of Administrative Pro
dure to keep administrative action constantly under revie

'arliamentary Commissioner has been appointed in Britain, on logy with the Scandinavian *Ombudsman*, to investigate com-nts against civil service administration.

'he most elaborate exposition of the case for formal control and variety of forms which it can assume is contained in C. S. ıeman's *Bureaucracy in a Democracy* (1950). He takes issue with :drich and similar theorists by arguing that the key condition democratic administration is the existence of authoritative ways nstructing officials. The authoritative bodies in the United :es are Congress and the president assisted by the central staff ıcies and the courts. Hyneman argues that the means of direc-. and control which are at their disposal are far more numerous effective, at least potentially, than is usually recognized to be case. Limits are set in prescribing the tasks of administration ch are made more real by specifying the nature of the organiza-required and the finance available. Control over appointments, ew and investigating procedures provide additional tools for task of ensuring democratic administration. Hyneman's outline ıe system of administrative direction and control in the United :es expresses fully the spirit of Herman Finer's view that onsibility is ensured through 'an arrangement of correction and ishment'.[21]

'he more extreme statements of the case for greater formal con-have often come in for severe criticism. E. Pendelton Herring ıks of how 'Lord Hewart looks with a futile nostalgia to the rule ıw as interpreted by the courts'.[22] But the more sophisticated onents of this case are not open to the charge that they fail to the inevitability of discretion and delegated legislation. In the ch for limits on these aspects of the official's power their exis-:e is admitted. However the very emphasis which is involved in quest for formal limits has been attacked as the wrong approach ıe problem of bureaucracy. Herbert Simon has expressed him-strongly and succinctly on this issue in commenting on the) Hoover Commission Report.[23] That report criticizes public ınistration in the United States for confused lines of authority consequent impairment of responsibility and accountability, also for lack of staff services. Simon argues that the existing agencies which provide 'independent' reviews of administra-action are themselves largely responsible for lack of clear lines ıthority. The establishment of such agencies involves increased operating costs, the development of a new interest group limits on operating departments which will manifest themselve red tape.

This criticism can be stated in more general terms. At the s plest, it poses the old question of '*Quis custodiet ipsos custodes?* the most complex level, it involves the general theory of the na and functioning of rules in social life. No rule applies itself. applied by men who have the twin tasks of interpreting its mea and assessing whether the empirical conditions exist to justify application. In other words, judgement must be exercised, every rule is dependent on the spirit in which this judgemer made. This leads some to argue that there cannot possibly 'neutral' administrators. For some the interpretation of a rule be too literal and reflect a spirit of red tape, for others that s interpretation will appear too loose and exhibit the official's at of power.[24] But if this dilemma exists for the official, it exists eq ly for those who are appointed to control officials. Even if those control officials are elected representatives, the results of persis examination of the extent to which officials adhere to rules very well be self-defeating, generating evasion, defensiveness only minimally satisfactory performance.

The resemblance of this argument among the democratic th ists to the criticisms which have been levelled at Max Weber is coincidental. C. J. Friedrich is an important figure in both a of controversy. In important respects the concept of democr administration which he advances is designed to be in direct op sition to Max Weber's account of purely rational administrat which is seen to correspond to the authoritarianism and legalis the German imperial civil service. Yet the remedies for bur cracy which he advocates also have characteristics which have b imputed to the more powerful continental civil services. In study of the Swiss civil service he proposes the active participa of civil servants in basic decision making in order to enhance t morale. He suggests 'partial self-government' in the servic inhibit undue public interference.[25] Elsewhere he insists that responsible administrator is one who is responsible both to pu sentiment and to technical knowledge. Neither of these factors be assured by decree.[26] They depend on the values and calibr the officials themselves.

It should now be apparent that the differing remedies offered

aucracy reflect some of the basic antitheses in social and poli-
science. In this argument there are echoes of the disputes
t the relative importance of formal and informal sources of
sion in organizations, punishment or treatment of criminals,
nissiveness or discipline in socialization, or, indeed, of force
onsensus as the basis of social order. The opponents of em-
is on formal controls in public administration are maintaining
if it is necessary for the individual to have personal autonomy
freedom of decision, and necessary for society that individuals
an inner commitment to democratic values, then no excep-
s can be made from these requirements in the case of public
ials and civil services.

he conclusion is that the commitment of the official to demo-
c values is a more important safeguard for democracy than any
al system of control. Methods of achieving this result include
ong emphasis on professional competence and a recruitment
y which both selects persons of the right calibre and ensures
their social background is such that they have a ready sym-
y for all sections of the community.[27] (It hardly needs mention
most social systems make these two aspects of recruitment
mpatible.) Professionalism and representativeness are expected
nhance public trust, and the result of this will be a decline in
demand for formal controls. But the beneficent effects do not
here. A decline in formal controls imposed from the outside
ts in a reduction of formal control within the official hierarchy.
official feels less threatened and trust between officials is en-
ed. B. H. Baum has concluded that decentralization depends
nutual trust.[28] But decentralization is associated with speed of
sion. This in turn reduces friction with the public and rein-
s public trust. The vicious circle of bureaucracy has become
gn.

one the less, it is possible to detect a note in this idea of
ocratic administration which seems dissonant. While the stress
responsiveness, this is achieved through autonomy. As has
been remarked, professionalism may enhance the listening
ty of the official, but it also increases his distance from the
ce of the noise.[29] It has been pointed out that American
ials are more representative of different strata of the population
congressmen are.[30] But they are still highly selected, and in the
er echelons have an educational and professional experience

which marks them off from the rest of the population. Re
writers, such as N. E. Long, W. S. Sayre and C. E. Jacob, a
unison in saying that the federal government service makes
fourth and equal arm of government.[31] P. Woll's remark is typ
'American bureaucracy takes its place as an equal partner wit
President, Congress and the judiciary.'[32] But if it is 'equal'
involved in a struggle for power with its equals. What relation,
do the other three arms of government bear to the public to w
the public service is so 'responsive'?

There would appear to be more to the criterion of responsive
than the internalization of democratic values by the official. T
indicated by Friedrich's remark: 'At best responsibility in a d
cracy will become fragmentary because of the indistinct voi
the principal whose agents the officials are supposed to be-
vast, heterogeneous masses composing the people.'[33] The
terms here are 'indistinct voice' and 'vast, heterogeneous ma
What is there to respond to? The implications are clearly se
Herring's *Public Administration and the Public Interest* (1936).
advocating responsiveness, he says that it is necessary to 'pro
a purpose of the state over and above the medley of interests
compose it'.[34] He gives this task to the officials and, thereby,
as perfect an evocation of Hegel's position as the changed
ditions of this century would allow.[35]

What the advocates of responsiveness have to offer may ap
strikingly similar to a characterization of bureaucracy which
suggested, 'a practice which keeps the citizens in a relation t
government like that of children to their guardians'.[36] The mo
public official is revealed as a paternalistic aristocrat. The p
speaks, yet it is the official who chooses when to listen, to w
and with what degree of attention. Mill saw a sharp conflic
tween bureaucracy and representative democracy. He saw
clear feature of the latter that it enhanced the capacity for pol
action and guaranteed the power of organized action being dif
in a community. It is this belief, that it is intrinsic to the id
democracy that the power of decision is not reserved to the
which sustains the third position on the problem of bureauc
which we identified. It is the foundation of the demands for ci
participation, workers' control or student power.[37] It has rece
no authoritative exposition.

To end this chapter on this note is to recall our discussion o ogists. The same theme appears: a hint of an emerging radical ission of the decision-making structure of the state and the nizations which dominate modern society. The separate treat- of the writers we have discussed in this chapter was justified eir critical posture towards both the facts and values they con- . But it is not unfair to comment that there are sufficient amined assumptions behind their arguments to warrant saying theirs is simply a sophisticated expression of the ideology of ern societies. It is regularly assumed that, while all men are bers of interest groups, a small number can see the interests of Democracy is held to be about this common interest: it has to do with the locus of political action. It is taken for granted the area of state action will continue to grow, that public als will increase in numbers, that their calibre must always be oved because their decisions are becoming more complex.

r the radical, it is precisely the ready acquiescence of the ern democratic theorists to this conceptual framework which etuates the modern problem of bureaucracy.

Conclusion: The Concept of Bureaucracy in Soci and Political Science

It has often been held against social scientists that invent unnecessary new terminology to conceal a poverty of i This may, on occasion, be a justified charge. But this study v seem to suggest a different failing. We have identified many d ent concepts being presented in the same verbal dress. The 'bureaucracy' has been applied to government by officials, p administration, the administration of any organization, admin tive efficiency or inefficiency, and the modern organization, to tion only some of the many concepts discussed. This appea evidence not an excess, but a poverty of terminological inver ness. Some explanation is necessary.

In the first place we should recall that each twist in the me of bureaucracy has had close affiliations with what went be This book will have failed if it has not succeeded in showin steps whereby 'bureaucracy' came to be applied to a ruling g of officials after it had referred to a method of governme officials; how it came to denote any rational administration a had referred to the system of modern administration; or h came to be used for any modern organization after being ap merely to the administrative sub-system. Each step of this kin proved intelligible. It is the end-product, a bevy of comp concepts, which is bewildering. Few concepts in social science undergone such a continual process of fragmentation and t formation. It is this which means that we are faced with much than the usual problem of discovering minor verbal disagreen and shifts of emphasis in the differing formulations of a conce

For the first part of a tentative explanation of this process consider some of the well-attested facts about the very are which concepts of bureaucracy have been applied. There are accounts of the growth of state power in the eighteenth centu the way government took on more and more functions in the teenth, and of the way this growth has been prolonged i

tieth.[1] An obvious indicator of this development is the growth
e percentage of the population who are employed in public
ces which has taken place in almost every decade in every
ty.[2] Similarly many sources tell us how organizations have
ased in number and size in modern society, and how, with
growth, there has been an increase in the proportion of
oyees who are engaged in administrative tasks.[3]

ese quantitative changes have been accompanied by qualita-
hanges in organizational structure, both in the case of govern-
and other organizations. A change which begins early in
strialized societies is the separation of domicile from place of
. This is accompanied by a separation of those who produce
those who own the product. These changes occupied the
tion of the nineteenth century. This century has been con-
d with a further separation: that between those who own and
who control the process of production. These 'separations'
sually expressed in terms particularly applicable to industry,
hey are equally appropriate to other sectors. For example, we
eplace the terms 'manager' and 'owner' by 'civil servant' and
ician', and discern the same process at work.

ciety now includes a distinct and recognizable group of man-
and administrators with similar job experiences, interests and
s. Their career structures, salaries and the qualifications de-
led of them are all special aspects of a wide range of adminis-
e techniques which are employed in both public and private
izations. Ideologies of 'good administration' help to stereo-
practices in all sectors and have an impact on the values of the
society. Finally, it is no longer possible for the citzen to
in aloof from these changes. He necessarily comes into contact
organizations in a wide range of everyday activities. That con-
s routinized and recorded to become both an element of
izational structure and a basic factor in the individual's
ience and outlook.

ese phenomena are central to our understanding of the speci-
tures of contemporary society. We may find isolated historical
pations, but fundamentally they are novel, and certainly they
w in the perception of the men who have observed and com-
d on them. Some facet of them has always been the focus of
ion for the writers we have been examining, and it is within
road context that ideas of bureaucracy have developed. The

term 'bureaucracy' was first used for novel features of governn
but as these were replaced in novelty by the successive change
have mentioned, the term was applied to the emergent feat
taking on new meanings even while the old usages were still cur
As a neologism, applied to a rapidly developing sector of mo
society, the conditions for a stabilization of its usage simply di
exist. With each major structural change there arose a
concept of bureaucracy.

It is possible to illustrate how this proliferation of concep
coupled with a preservation of terminology. Let us conside
concept of bureaucracy as government by officials. It ma
broadly conceived, and held to comprise a range of features su
a hierarchic chain of offices, specific appointment procedures,
phasis on written regulations, set administrative routines, di
tionary powers for officials and their exercise of state coer
The relative emphasis given to the various features of the
cept may not be explicitly stated, and may vary with per
interpretation.

Now let us consider what happens to this concept when or
zations develop which have many of these characteristics: hiera
appointing procedures, etc. They may differ from what has hit
been called bureaucracy in one respect only—the exercise of
coercion. But, although this was never explicit, many users o
concept may have regarded the aspect of coercion as unimpo
The similarity between governmental and non-governm
organization in respect of the other features may be so great
for these people, there will appear to be no reason for withho
the designation 'bureaucracy' from the latter while giving it t
former.

But this conceptual development will not satisfy those who re
the use of state coercion by officials as an intrinsic part of the
of bureaucracy. The designation of non-governmental orga
tions as bureaucracies incites them to make explicit their
emphasis on the importance of state coercion. They now pre
regard as contingent the other features of bureaucracy which
sioned the extension of the concept to non-governmental orga
tions. The result is two competing concepts of bureaucracy
referring to the structure of organizations generally, the oth
governments where officials exercise state power. At the same
the original concept will still have its adherents.

his account is a fair paradigm of the processes of thought ined in the preceding chapters, we may identify two basic dients in the development of ideas on bureaucracy. The first is ıd concept with vague outline. A new identifying label such as aucracy' will be symptomatic of the lack of time which has ed for agreement to emerge on the concept's scope (although s true only where there is no authoritative invention and ition of the term). The second ingredient is that the situation ı is being conceptualized should itself be changing and ing into qualitatively quite different forms.

is combination of social and ideal factors may be held to pro- a reasonably satisfying explanation of the process we may call inological conservation and conceptual change'. We could ılate further and argue that social change is itself so disturbing it is necessary to the individual that at least the illusion of rity is provided by the conservation of terminology. But it ld be idle to speculate on the psychological functions of this ess. What we can see is that there is no inherent reason for the ess to come to a halt. Only a general consciousness of the fac- involved in conceptual development and a determination to ways of improving the precision of our thinking about society assist. It is to be hoped that this book may play some small part is, and that the reader may now be able to pick his way more y through the conceptual thickets which the term 'bureaucracy' eals.

ut enhanced consciousness, though an aid, does not of itself e the immediate problem of the working social scientist. He es about men who speak of bureaucracy in their daily lives and eads the products of scholars who write about bureaucracy. He ill faced with the choice of a conceptual strategy when dealing ı the phenomena to which the term 'bureaucracy' has been lied. It would, of course, be totally contrary to the spirit of the ceding account for this writer to attempt to offer an 'authori- ve' new definition of bureaucracy. All that has gone before uld indicate that this would be nugatory and self-defeating. But ıe comments on the respective merits of differing conceptual ıtegies may be in order.

f we consider the concepts we have reviewed in terms of their ıeral use and acceptability, one factor stands out. The more arly a concept has been articulated with a general conceptual framework, the greater likelihood it has of penetrating int thinking of social scientists. Max Weber's, Harold Lasswel even John Stuart Mill's ideas of bureaucracy are not whims moment but are supported by a range of other concepts whi a large extent, stand or fall together. A counsel of perfection would-be producer of the ultimate definition of bureaucracy well be to ensure that his concept was part of a total and cor hensive conceptual framework for social science. But to tal such a task can only be viewed as quixotic. The number of frameworks in existence seems to suggest that each new schem only be an addition to, rather than a replacement of, what already. Moreover, as we have seen, social change involves a stant revision of concepts and it is difficult to envisage any fina authoritative conceptual scheme.

A radically different approach is to consider the term 'bu cracy' as it is used in everyday speech. Its wide currency has remarked on ever since the 1840s. Social life is depende shared concepts and it may be felt that there is bound to be cient consensus about the meaning of bureaucracy in po parlance to warrant acceptance of this concept by social scie The difficulties here are notorious. It is by no means certai the popular use of the term invariably has an empirical refere may be no more informative than any other expostulation of a in which the use of words indicates more about the state o individual using them than any aspect of a perceived situation even if we concentrate on those occasions when the term does clearly to an aspect of social life, we are faced with the same lem as we meet with in the most sophisticated social science con For social science and social life are not hermetically seale from each other. We must expect the usages of academic discu to percolate into everyday language, and we cannot anticipate neutral arbitration between them.

A third strategy is designed to do precisely this—to prov middle course between the various concepts. It was employ the very first academic scrutiny of the concept of bureaucrac 1846 Robert von Mohl expressed his concern at the varying us the term 'bureaucracy'. Everyone, he said, is talking about i no one appears to have given it thought. Many people, he tho use it to demonstrate their intelligence, or to give the impressi insight and political sophistication. 'In these circumstances

approach to a clear idea of this frequently used but ill-
d concept is to compile as comprehensive a list as possible of
rious accounts of the tendencies and consequences of bureau-
'[4] He hoped to devise a definition, as a result of this compila-
which included only those elements on which there was
l agreement.

s method still has its adherents, and we have come across
les of it.[5] But its successful employment is dependent on the
y of a basic assumption, which is that the varying definitions
rm are simply different attempts to sum up the specific nature
same range of objects (*denotata*). Put in other terms, the pre-
s that different writers on bureaucracy are talking about the
thing and merely disagree on the appropriate language for
bing it. Now if the account in this book is correct such an
ption must be invalid in the case of bureaucracy. For we
ound quite distinct concepts using that name. Certainly these
pts overlap and we have concentrated on showing how they
ated, logically and historically. But there is no element com-
o them all which could form part of a useful definition.

arly there seems to be only one possible approach left. This is
id the use of the term 'bureaucracy' while pursuing research
areas in which it has been employed, for nothing in this book
l be thought to diminish the importance of such work. Indeed
riter hopes that such conceptual clarification as he may have
ed will contribute to the success of future research. Such a
can, without doubt, save much confusion. But it is possible
vage something small from the wrecks of these conceptual
gies. When we say that the concepts we have discussed are
l, we may have found the major information function which
rm 'bureaucracy' has.

identify different groups of related human beings we have
names. They are devoid of meaning, but none the less use-
the same way 'bureaucracy' is useful in identifying a range
ated problems, i.e. the whole gamut of issues concerning the
ns of individuals to abstract organizational features. We can-
xpect this name to tell us anything more than the fact of
nship, of historical and logical connection between these
ems. But that single piece of information is important enough,
ademics and citizens alike.

Notes and References

'ull publication details of works cited will be found in the Bibliography.

ntroduction

liamentary Debates, House of Commons Official Report, Vol. 757, no. 48, uary 29, 1968, col. 885, 'Growth of Bureaucracy'.

d., col. 967. The speaker was Mr J. W. Pardoe, Liberal member for nwall, North.

d., col. 980. Mr George Lawson, Labour member for Motherwell, reply- to Sir Harmar Nicholls, Conservative member for Peterborough.

R. Sharp, "La Développement de la Bureaucratie aux États-Unis", *ue des Sciences Politiques*, Vol. 50, 1927, p. 394.

Morstein Marx, 'Bureaucracy and Consultation', *Review of Politics*, Vol. 939, p. 87.

Reader in Bureaucracy, edited by R. K. Merton et al., 1952, and *Bureau- cy and Bureaucratization*, a trend report and bibliography by S. N. enstadt, 1958.

1/The Emergence of the Concept

icent de Gournay (1712–59) translated influential writers on economics, h as Child and Culpepper, into French. Himself an *intendant du com- rce*, he was an important member of the group of economists known as Physiocrats. For biographical details see G. Schelle, *Vincent de Gournay*, 7.

con de Grimm and Diderot, *Correspondance, Littéraire, Philosphique et itique*, 1753–69, 1813 edn, Vol. 4, p. 146. De Gournay's verbal inventive- s appears to have been considerable. The slogan, '*laissez faire, laissez ser*', has also been attributed to him.

d., p. 508. Letter of July 15, 1765.

Warnotte in "Bureaucratie et Fonctionnairisme", 1937, recounts that de urnay invented the term after a visit to Hamburg in 1745 but gives no rce for this story.

Machiavelli, *The Prince*, Ch. 22.

e H. G. Creel, "The Beginnings of Bureaucracy in China: The Origin the Hsien", 1964.

ctionnaire de la Langue Française, Supplément, 1798.

H. Campe, *Wörterbuch zu Erklärung und Verdeutschung der unseren rache aufgedrungenen fremden Ausdrücke*, Braunschweig 1813, p. 161.

A. Marchi, *Dizionario Technico-Etimilogico-Filologico*, Milan 1828, p. 138.

noré de Balzac, *Les Employés*, 1836, translated by E. Marriage as *reaucracy*, 1898, p. 84.

Le Play, *La Réforme Sociale en France*, 1864, p. 237.

Littré, *Dictionnaire de la Langue Française*, Hachette, Paris 1873.

Block, *Petit Dictionnaire Politique et Social*, Perrin, Paris, 1896, p. 94.

Schulz, *Deutsches Fremdwörterbuch*, Trübner, Strassburg 1913, p. 102.

15 C. J. Kraus, *Vermischte Schriften*, Nicolovius, Königsberg 1808, p.
16 W. von Humboldt, *Ideen zu einem Versuch die Gränzen der Wirksam Staats zu bestimmen*, first published 1851.
17 *Die Briefe des Freiherrn von Stein an den Freiherrn von Gagern 181* Cotta, Stuttgart 1833, pp. 90–2, letter of August 24, 1821.
18 K. Heinzen, *Die Preussische Büreaukratie*, 1845, p. 11. It is worth Stein's emphasis on the caste nature of the bureaucrats. Marx was with Heinzen's work and would have come across this passage by Heinzen, if not in the original.
19 J. J. von Görres, *Europa und die Revolution*, 1821, p. 149.
20 J. J. von Görres, *Deutschland und die Revolution*, 1819.
21 In the translation by J. Black (Longmans, London 1820) it was ren 'regulated on the principle of offices or bureaus' (p. 253). In the ano translation in *The Pamphleteer* (London 1820), it was omitted abridgement.
22 *Tour in England, Ireland, and France*, by a German Prince (Prin Pückler-Muskau), tr. by Mrs S. Austen, Effingham, Wilson, Londo p. 34.
23 *The Popular Encyclopaedia*, Blackie, Glasgow 1837, p. 755.
24 Thomas Carlyle, *Latter Day Pamphlets*, No. IV, "The New D Street", April 15, 1850, in *Collected Works*, Vol. 19, Chapman an London 1870, p. 173.
25 H. Spencer, *The Study of Sociology*, 1st edn 1837; 1961, p. 111.
26 Arnout O'Donnel, "State Education in France", p. 583.
27 J. S. Blackie, "Prussia and the Prussian System", passim.
28 J. S. Mill, *Principles of Political Economy*, Vol. 2, p. 528.
29 J. S. Mill, *On Liberty*, 1892 edn, p. 66.
30 J. S. Mill, *Considerations on Representative Government*, p. 113.
31 Ibid., p. 114.
32 Ibid., p. 115.
33 Ibid., p. 117.
34 W. Bagehot, *The English Constitution*, 1963 edn, p. 197.
35 Ibid., p. 198.
36 E. Fischel, *Die Verfassung Englands*, 1862, pp. 132–6 and 249–52.
37 F. von Schulte, "Bureaucracy and its Operation in Germany and Hungary", p. 456.
38 Ibid., p. 432.
39 Ibid., p. 458.
40 Ibid., p. 433.
41 See A. Lang, *Life, Letters and Diaries of Sir Stafford Northcote*, Blac Edinburgh and London 1890, Vol. 2, p. 219.
42 Published in book form the following year as *The Man versus the Sta* were entitled "The New Toryism", "The Coming Slavery", "The the Legislators", and "The Great Political Superstition".
43 H. Spencer, *The Man versus the State*, p. 33. In an essay of 1871, alized Administration", Spencer outlined his theory of the negative the state and his absolute opposition to positive interference.
44 F. C. Montague, *The Limits of Individual Liberty*, p. 229.
45 A. S. Green, "Growing Bureaucracy and Parliamentary Decline",
46 "The Encroaching Bureaucracy" (anonymous), *The Quarterly* 1917, p. 52.
47 J. Ramsay Muir, *Peers and Bureaucrats*, p. 8.
48 Ibid., p. 14.

., p. 22.
on Stein, *Die Verwaltungslehre*, 2nd edn 1869, p. 14.
ood source in English is H. C. Johnson's "Concept of Bureaucracy in
neralism", 1964. This is somewhat unhappily titled since, as the author
es, the term 'bureaucracy' was not current in the writing he discusses,
indeed the German concept of bureaucracy was developed to highlight
ntrast with cameralist thinking.
in particular the frequently cited text by a Westphalian finance minister,
A. von Malchus, *Politik der inneren Staatsverwaltung*, 1823, especially
5–8.
gemeine deutsche Real-Encyclopaedie oder Conversationslexikon, Brock-
us, Leipzig, 5th edn 1819, Vol. 2, p. 158.
inzen, op. cit., p. 12.
Rohmer, *Deutschlands alte und neue Bureaukratie*, 1848, p. 1. An anony-
us article of 1857, "Der bureaukratische Staat nach seinem Ausgangs-
nkt und Ziel", offered yet another solution to bureaucracy in the form of
ociety based on professional groups.
, for instance, in *Das Staatslexicon*, edited by K. von Rotteck and K.
elcker, 1859, and *Deutsches Staatswörterbuch*, edited by J. C. Bluntschli
d K. Brater, 1857.
nversationslexicon, Brockhaus, Leipzig 1864, Vol. 3, pp. 873–4.
ein, op. cit., p. 287.
von Mohl, "Ueber Bureaukratie", 1862 edn, claims that after 1846
eryone began to discuss this topic.
id., p. 108.
, Brater, in Bluntschli and Brater, op. cit., p. 294 strongly deprecated this
age.
Olszewski, *Bureaukratie*, 1904. This volume has gone unnoticed in the
nglo-Saxon literature. It appears to be the first separate volume devoted
holly to the topic of bureaucracy, but a full length study entitled "La
urocrazia e il Governo Parlamentare", by I. Santangelo Spoto appeared
vo years earlier in the *Biblioteca di Scienze Politiche e Amministrative*, edited
y A. Brunialti. Relying largely on the sources discussed in this chapter,
his study is concerned with the genesis and structure of bureaucracy, its
rganization in Italy and France, its reform, and the idea of responsible
ureaucracy.
. Le Play, op. cit., pp. 236–5.
'or instance L. Vivien's *Études Administratives*, 1845, makes no reference
o the problem.
. de Tocqueville, *L'Ancien Régime et la Révolution*, 8th edn 1877, p. 246.
. Leroy-Beaulieu, *L'État Moderne et ses Fonctions*, especially p. 49 and
p. 80–8.

2/The Classical Formulations

The edition was dated 1896.
In his *Sulla Teorica dei Governi e sul Governo Parlamentare*, 1884, Ch. 1.
Ibid., p. 18.
Storia delle Dottrine Politiche, 1933, Ch. 40. An English translation of this
chapter is given by J. H. Meisel at the end of *The Myth of the Ruling Class*,
1958.
See "The Anti-Aristotelianism of Gaetano Mosca and its Fate", by R.
Sereno in *Ethics*, Vol. 48, 1937–38.

6 *Sulla Teorica*, p. 19 as translated by Meisel, op. cit., p. 32.
7 In the *Storia* he added the city state to make a third type.
8 The importance Mosca attached to bureaucracy was a feature of *Th Class* which represented a novel development compared with hi *Sulla Teorica*. As Meisel (op. cit., p. 137), says, it was introducec suddenly'. It is not possible to ascertain what, if any, new influen affected Mosca.
9 The last six chapters of the English edition of *The Ruling Class* were in 1920–23. These were especially marked by their opposition to cratic rule, but it is also evident in the earlier chapters.
10 *The Ruling Class*, pp. 142–3. Subsequently (p. 284) Mosca said, 'Con and collectivist societies would beyond any doubt be managed by o This successful prediction should encourage all who despair of t dictive powers of social science.
11 Ibid., p. 134.
12 Ibid., p. 269.
13 As Meisel points out (op. cit., pp. 196–206) Mosca never bothered t bureaucracy and he neglected Max Weber and his school.
14 Mosca, op. cit., pp. 83–4.
15 Published in German as *Zur Soziologie des Parteiwesens in der m Demokratie.*
16 Mosca, op. cit., p. 365.
17 Ibid., p. 338.
18 The fatalism of Michels's approach as compared with Mosca's was r in their political careers. Believing oligarchy inevitable Michels sup the Fascists in Italy, whereas Mosca never joined them.
19 See above, p. 32.
20 The best account of Weber's substantive sociological work is that Bendix, *Max Weber, An Intellectual Portrait*, 1960.
21 The first, "Wesen, Voraussetzungen und Entfaltung der bürokrat Herrschaft", stemmed from the years 1911–13 and appeared on pp. 5 of *Wirtschaft und Gesellschaft* 4th edn (cited henceforward as *WuG*). been translated by H. H. Gerth and C. Wright Mills on pp. 196–244 o selection *From Max Weber: Essays in Sociology*, 1948. The second, w between 1918–20, appeared in *WuG*, pp. 125–30. It has been translat A. M. Henderson and T. Parsons in *The Theory of Social and Eco Organisation*, 1947, pp. 329–41.
22 "Parlament und Regierung im neugeordneten Deutschland", was rep in Max Weber's *Gesammelte Politische Schriften*, 2nd edn 1958, pp. 29 (henceforward referred to as *GPS*).
23 A very recent example of emphasis upon the methodology of We writing on bureaucracy is N. Mouzelis, *Organization and Bureaucracy*, For an article interpreting Weber's theory as an expression of a philo of history see A. Gouldner, "Metaphysical Pathos and the Theo Bureaucracy", *American Political Science Review*, Vol. 49, 1955. This will be discussed further in the next chapter.
24 In Henderson and Parsons, op. cit., see pp. 145–52.
25 Henderson and Parsons translate *Verband* as 'corporate group'. This so too legalistic to this writer. *Verband* is as common a term in Germ organization is in English.
26 Henderson and Parsons, op. cit., p. 150.
27 Ibid., p. 146.

'uG, p. 545. Cf. M. Rheinstein, *Max Weber on Law in Economy and Society*, 54, p. 330.
enderson and Parsons, op. cit., p. 152. Parsons notes 'the term *Herrschaft* s no satisfactory English equivalent'. Rheinstein prefers to translate it as omination'. The nearest translation is 'rule' as in 'rule of kings', but fortunately 'rule' has another meaning as in of 'rules of the game'. uthority' seems the best translation since Weber himself, *WuG*, p. 544 ed *Autoritat* as a synonym for his special meaning of *Herrschaft*.
'uG, p. 28. Cf. Henderson and Parsons, op. cit., p. 152.
'uG, p. 28.
heinstein, op. cit., p. 330, *WuG*, p. 541.
'uG, p. 28, Henderson and Parsons, op. cit., p. 152.
'uG, p. 548, translated in Rheinstein, op. cit., p. 334. He referred to 'the -called "advantage of the small number" '.
'uG, p. 153. Cf. Henderson and Parsons, op. cit., p. 382.
eber outlined this scheme several times: *WuG*, pp. 122–57, translated by enderson and Parsons, op. cit., pp. 324–92; *WuG*, pp. 549–50, translated Rheinstein, op. cit., pp. 336–7; *WuG*, pp. 551–8.
g. *WuG*, p. 126, p. 550.
uG, p. 127; Henderson and Parsons, op. cit., p. 335; *GPS*, p. 319.
g. *WuG*, pp. 126, 552.
PS, pp. 308–10.
'uG, p. 552.
'uG, p. 552.
very good, brief summary of these is available in R. Aron, *Main Currents Sociological Thought*, Vol. 2, 1967, pp. 197–204.
ne following version of Weber's ideal typical formulation on legal authority d a bureaucratic administrative staff is taken from *WuG*, pp. 124–8. For translation see Henderson and Parsons, op. cit., pp. 329–34.
hese propositions are also set out in abbreviated form.
uG, pp. 126–7; Henderson and Parsons, op. cit., p. 334.
'uG, p. 128; Henderson and Parsons, op. cit., p. 337.
g. *GPS*, pp. 318, 321.
PS, p. 310.
'uG, pp. 154, 564.
id., pp. 158–76; Henderson and Parsons, op. cit., pp. 392–423. These ere apart from the legal definition of the rights and duties of the bureau- ats.
s early as 1895, in his inaugural lecture, Weber had taken 'national power' a political good of paramount importance. The extent of Weber's tionalism and responsibility for later developments in Germany have come a matter for heated debate.

3/The Debate with Weber

or an account see A. Oberschall, *Empirical Social Research in Germany, 48–1914*, pp. 134–6, where the author also refers to Weber's non-ideal pe of bureaucracy.
Il Pensiero Moderno, Vol. 1, 1912, pp. 310–16, cited by J. H. Meisel, . cit.
om Max Weber, edited by H. H. Gerth and C. Wright Mills, 1948, p. 232.
id., p. 232. A good account of the careful consideration Weber gave to the oblem of power and bureaucracy is A. Diamant's "The Bureaucratic

Model: Max Weber Rejected, Rediscovered, Reformed", in *Pa Comparative Public Administration*, edited by F. Heady and S. L. 1962.

5 "Die Behördenorganisation und die allgemeine Staatsverwaltung Pr im 18 Jahrhundert", in *Acta Borussica*, Vol. 1 and "Der deutsche Be staat vom 16 bis 18 Jahrhundert", in *Umrisse und Untersuchung Verfassungs- Verwaltungs- und Wirtschaftsgeschichte*, 1898.

6 Schmoller, "Die Behördenorganisation", p. 31 (this author's transl

7 Ibid., p. 32.

8 E. Strauss, *The Ruling Servants*, 1961, pp. 40–1.

9 Available in his *Reader in Bureaucracy*, 1952, pp. 361–71.

10 Ibid., p. 362.

11 The major statement of his theory is in *TVA and the Grass Roots*, 19 earlier version is contained in his "An Approach to a Theory of F cracy", in the *American Sociological Review*, 1943.

12 For a useful account of these see G. Friedman, *Industrial Society*,

13 Henderson and Parsons, op. cit., pp. 58–60.

14 Gouldner also mentions a third type, mock-bureaucracy, where th are not taken seriously by any of the participants.

15 In *Verfassung und Verfassungsrecht*, reprinted in *Staats rechtliche A lungen und andere Aufsätze*, 1955, p. 30 (this author's translation).

16 See "Bureaucracy: the Problem and its Setting", in the *America ological Review*, 1947.

17 R. Bendix, *Higher Civil Servants in American Society*, p. 12.

18 "Some Observations on Weber's Analysis of Bureaucracy", in Merton, *Reader in Bureaucracy*, 1952, p. 31.

19 "Theoretical Limitations of Max Weber's Systematic Analysis of cracy", in the *Philippine Journal of Public Administration*, 1957.

20 P. M. Blau, *The Dynamics of Bureaucracy*, p. 201.

21 "Bureaucratic and Craft Administration of Production: A Comp Study", *Administrative Science Quarterly*, 1959–60.

22 See G. Sjöberg, R. A. Brymer and B. Farris, "Bureaucracy and the Class", in *Sociology and Social Research*, 1966.

23 See E. Litwak and H. J. Meyer, "A Balance Theory of Co-ordinat tween Bureaucratic Organisations and Community Primary Grou *Administrative Science Quarterly*, 1966–67.

24 In "Weberian v. Welfare Bureaucracy in Traditional Society", *A trative Science Quarterly*, 1961–62.

25 "The Development and Decline of Patrimonial and Bureaucratic A trations", *Administrative Science Quarterly*, 1962–63.

26 See his introduction to that volume, "An Overview of Bureaucra Political Development".

27 "Metaphysical Pathos and the Theory of Bureaucracy", *American Science Review*, 1955.

28 "Max Weber's Two Conceptions of Bureaucracy", *American Jou Sociology*, 1957–58.

29 "Max Weber et La Russie", *Le Contrat Social*, 1960. Similarly F. S has argued that Weber would not have been able to account for th party's subversion of the German civil service (in "Bureaucra National Socialism: A Reconsideration of Weberian Theory", in Merton's *Reader in Bureaucracy*, 1952).

30 "The Beginnings of Bureaucracy in China: The Origin of the *Journal of Asian Studies*, 1964.

The Bureaucrat as Pro-Consul: The Restoration Prefect and the Police enerale", *Comparative Studies in Society and History*, 1965.

. Berger, *Bureaucracy and Society in Modern Egypt*, 1957 and C. Beck, ureaucracy and Political Development in Eastern Europe" in La Palomra, op. cit., 1963.

e above, note 18.

s examples of this point of view one may mention S. R. Udy, "Bureauacy and Rationality in Weber's Organisation Theory", *American Sociogical Review*, 1959; R. H. Hall, "The Concept of Bureaucracy—an npirical Assessment", *American Journal of Sociology*, 1963; C. R. Hinings al., "An Approach to the Study of Bureaucracy", *Sociology*, 1967.

au and Scott, op. cit., p. 534.

or a more recent restatement of this view see N. Mouzelis, *Organisation d Bureaucracy*, 1967.

arch and Simon, op. cit., p. 36.

G. Francis and R. C. Stone, *Service and Procedure in Bureaucracy*, 7.

ouzelis, op. cit., p. 51.

Max Weber's Ideal typus der Bürokratie und die Organisationssoziologie", ölner *Zeitschrift für Soziologie und Sozialpsychologie*, 1965.

Rationality" or a cognate term appears on twenty-three occasions even in e briefest of Weber's three essays on bureaucracy.

uG, p. 124; Henderson and Parsons, op. cit., p. 328.

uG, p. 125; Henderson and Parsons, op. cit., p. 329. This was the first of eber's five propositions on the basis of legal authority (see above p. 43).

eber used his two technical terms, *Zweckrationalität* (purposive rationaty) and *Wertrationalitat* (value rationality), to express the difference etween laws which were means to ends and laws which were the direct nbodiment of values.

uG, p. 125; Henderson and Parsons, op. cit., p. 330. This was the second his five propositions.

uG, p. 125; Henderson and Parsons, op. cit., p. 330. This was the fifth of e five propositions.

uG, p. 126; Henderson and Parson, op. cit., 331. Parson notes that he nds this distinction unclarified by Weber. It is best understood as the stitutional counterpart of Weber's two types of rational action.

uG, p. 126; Henderson and Parsons, op. cit., p. 331.

uG, p. 129; Henderson and Parsons, op. cit., p. 339.

uG, p. 141; Henderson and Parsons, op. cit., p. 361.

his was especially true of the Germany of Weber's time. Even today the ajority of higher civil servants in Germany are trained lawyers. But, of ourse, even in countries without systems of administrative law the interetation of laws and regulations is an important part of administrative tivity.

eber sometimes termed this the 'paradox of consequences' (*Paradoxie der olgen*). Merton's "Bureaucratic Structure and Personality" does at least knowledge the importance of this idea and Weber's emphasis on it. It is onic that it should have been used in criticism of Weber.

ee E. Baumgarten, *Max Weber: Werk und Person*, 1964, p. 514.

id., p. 516.

is, therefore, not without significance that Mayntz (see above, note 40), nds it necessary to attribute to Weber a concern for '*Effizienz*', a word he id not use.

55 A good example of the over-eagerness of writers in English to m issue out of Weber's supposed concern for efficiency is provided by C ner in the introduction to *Patterns of Industrial Bureaucracy*, pp. 19– assumes Weber was discussing what made bureaucracy effective. B quotation he takes for criticism involves an altogether unwarranted in of the idea of effectiveness by the translator.

56 For a discussion of the difficulties see the entry on 'efficiency' in *A D ary of the Social Sciences*, edited by J. Gould and W. L. Kolb, 1964.

57 Implicit in Weber's distinction was the difference between the ration thought and the rationality of conduct. A similar distinction in a di context has recently been made by I. C. Jarvie and J. Agassi, "The P of the Rationality of Magic" in the *British Journal of Sociology*, 1967

58 See above, p. 61.

59 Thus Weber viewed the Taylor theories of management as a contri to rationalizing production. See Henderson and Parsons, op. cit., p.

60 See "Der Beamte", an essay reprinted in *Ideen zur Stats-und K zoziologie*, 1927.

61 The best statement of Weber's position is contained in Herbert S essay "Bürokratie und Politische Machtbildung", 1955. He makes a of explaining the small part the problem of inefficiency played in W conceptualization of bureaucracy.

4/Bureaucracy and the Ideologists

1 In the *Marx-Engels Gesamtausgabe* (henceforward cited as MEGA), Sec Vol. 1. The relevant section, "Die Regierungsgewalt", is on pp. 448

2 Hegel's *Philosophy of Right*, translated by T. M. Knox, 1942, p. 193

3 P. Naville, *Le Nouveau Leviathan*, 1957, p. 98.

4 MEGA, p. 456: 'The bureaucratic spirit is an out and out jesuitical, theo spirit. The bureaucrats are the state Jesuits and state theologians. B cracy is *la république pretre*.'

5 Ibid., p. 457.

6 K. Marx and F. Engels, *The German Ideology*, p. 78.

7 In *Marx and Engels: Basic Writings on Politics and Philosophy*, edi L. S. Feuer, 1959, p. 29.

8 Ibid., p. 127.

9 Ibid., p. 456. For Heinzen, see above Ch. 1, p. 28.

10 Naville, op. cit., p. 101, says that at this stage Marx was still a democr not yet a communist.

11 Marx and Engels, *The German Ideology*, pp. 208–9.

12 In an article in the *Neue Rheinische Zeitung*, November 12, 1848, Kontrerevolution in Berlin", reprinted in MEGA, Section 7, Vol. 1,

13 Feuer, op. cit., p. 343.

14 Ibid., p. 343.

15 Ibid., p. 29.

16 For Bakunin's views on bureaucracy see G. P. Maximoff, *The P Philosophy of Bakunin: Scientific Anarchism.*

17 K. Wittfogel, "The Ruling Bureaucracy of Oriental Despotism. A P menon that Paralyzed Marx", *Review of Politics*, Vol. 15, 1953. S. A *The Social and Political Thought of Karl Marx*, 1968, p. 51, reco instance where Marx spoke of India being ruled by a bureaucracy. B is insufficient to warrant rejecting Wittfogel's interpretation, wh shared by G. Lichtheim, *Marxism*, 1961, p. 384.

)ne Step Forward, Two Steps Back, quoted in T. Anderson, *Masters of Russian Marxism*, 1963, p. 66.

)ie Voraussetzungen des Sozialismus und die Aufgaben der Sozialdemokratie, 899, translated as *Evolutionary Socialism*, 1909, p. 55.

Leninism or Marxism?", 1904, in *The Russian Revolution and Leninism and Marxism*, edited by B. D. Wolfe, 1961, p. 102.

bid., "The Russian Revolution", 1918, p. 71.

The Labour Revolution, 1925, includes a chapter devoted to bureaucracy.

Collected Works, Vol. 25, 1964, pp. 486–7.

bid., p. 481.

bid., pp. 486–7.

ee R. V. Daniels, *The Conscience of the Revolution: Communist Opposition in Soviet Russia*, 1960, pp. 115–8.

bid., p. 145.

ee T. Anderson, op. cit., pp. 179–88.

ee A. G. Meyer, *Leninism*, 1957, p. 214.

. Stalin, *Leninism*, 1928, Vol. 2, pp. 372–3.

ee A. Brumberg, "Soviet Campaign against Survivals of Capitalism", *Russian Review*, Vol. 12, 1953.

ee K. P. Mangold, "Lenin's Cardinal Rules of Poverty and Recall: Neg-ected Ideological Weapons for the West", *Orbis*, Vol. 8, 1964–5.

IEGA, Section 1, Vol. III, "Kritische Randglossen zu dem Artikel: 'Der König om Preussen und die Sozialreform. Von einem Preussen' ", 1844, p. 14.

G. D. H. Cole sees bureaucratization as the real issue between Trotsky and Stalin in his *History of Socialist Thought*, Vol. 4, 1963, p. 861.

The New Course, translated by M. Schachtman, 1943, pp. 50–1.

The Revolution Betrayed, p. 235.

ublished under the pseudonym Bruno R.

ublished in a collected edition as *The Bureaucratic Revolution: The Rise of the Stalinist State*, 1962.

Mussolini's and Hitler's regimes have come to be essentially similar to Stalin's. . . . The rest is choreography.' Rizzi, op. cit., p. 314.

This did not prevent Rizzi from calling for a proletarian revolution to eplace the existing bureaucracy with a new directing class.

See J. Djordevic, "Local Self-Government in Yugoslavia", *American Slavic and East European Review*, Vol. 12, 1953.

State and Law: Soviet and Yugoslav Theory, 1964, p. 50.

The Thoughts of Chairman Mao Tse-tung, 1967, especially pp. 24, 30, 35, 4–5, 80 and 174. Chen Po-Ta, in *Mao Tse-tung on the Chinese Revolution*, 953, pp. 25–6, notes the importance of the element 'bureaucratic-capita-ism' in Mao's revolutionary formula.

See *Cuba, Socialisme et Développement*, 1964, p. 108. He has also written on he theme of Cuba and bureaucracy in *Lands Alive*, 1965, Ch. 7.

As reported by Theodore Draper, *Castroism, Theory and Practice*, 1965, pp. 192–7, where he gives an account of the dispute between a French Communist, Charles Bettelheim, and Che Guevara.

Marxism in Modern France, 1966, pp. 182–90.

See J. Sauvageot, A. Geismar, D. Cohn-Bendit, and J.-P. Duteuil, *The Student Revolt*, 1968, p. 60. Geismar is speaking.

bid., p. 79.

For the United States see *The New Radicals*, edited by P. Jacobs and S. Landau, 1966, especially the sixth section, "The FSM—Revolt against Liberal Bureaucracy".

50 An additional exception can be made of Bukharin who was familiar some sociology, in particular that of Michels. The nearest approach critical analysis of the concept of bureaucracy among Marxists is found in André Stawar's *Libres Essais Marxistes*, 1963. His essay Bureaucratie Soviétique" dates from 1934. He was under the surveil of both his own government in Poland and the Stalinists.

51 Good accounts of the response of the Fascists to bureaucracy will be f in S. Neumann, *Permanent Revolution*, 1942; Franz Neumann, *Behe The Structure and Practice of National Socialism*, 1942; F. Morstein M "Bureaucracy and Dictatorship", *Review of Politics*, 1941.

52 This is the view of Franz Neumann, op. cit., p. 39.

53 B. Mussolini, *The Doctrine of Fascism*, 1935, p. 12.

54 A. Hitler, *Mein Kampf*, p. 154. Similar statements can also be fou Alfred Rosenberg's work, e.g. in *Der Mythus des 20 Jahrhunderts*, 1943 edn, p. 526.

55 Quoted by Franz Neumann, op. cit., p. 68.

56 B. Mussolini, *My Autobiography*, n.d., p. 268.

57 B. Mussolini, *The Corporate State*, 1938, p. 28.

58 For an account of Mussolini's methods see T. Cole, "Italy's Fascist Bu cracy", *American Political Science Review*, 1938.

59 B. Mussolini, *The Corporate State*, p. 46. Both capitalist and soc systems were going in this direction according to Mussolini; somethi an anticipation of Rizzi's position.

60 Hitler, op. cit., pp. 119, 156–7.

61 See for example F. Morstein Marx, "German Bureaucracy in Transit *American Political Science Review*, 1934; F. S. Burin, "Bureaucracy National Socialism—a Reconsideration of Weberian Theory", in R Merton et al., *Reader in Bureaucracy*, 1952.

62 *Blut und Ehre*, 1936, Vol. 2, p. 68.

63 See his "Legalität und Legitimität", 1932, reprinted in *Verfassungs liche Aufsätze 1924–54*, 1958.

64 Examples include J. M. Beck, *Our Wonderland of Bureaucracy*, 1932; Crider, *The Bureaucrat*, 1944; L. Sullivan, *The Dead Hand of Bureauc* 1940; and *Bureaucracy Runs Amuck*, 1944.

65 E. Pendelton Herring, *Public Administration and the Public Interest*, p Hermann Finer, "Critics of 'Bureaucracy' ", *Political Science Quar* 1945, also attacks these writers on bureaucracy for their indiscriminat of the term.

66 L. von Mises, *Bureaucracy*, 1946, p.2.

67 J. A. Schumpeter, *Capitalism, Socialism and Democracy*, third edn p. 206.

68 For a good survey of the attitudes of various socialists to bureaucrac R. Bendix, "Socialism and the Theory of Bureaucracy", *Canadian Jo of Economic and Political Science*, 1950. A book as influential as C. A Crosland's *The Future of Socialism*, 1956, omits any discussion of the prob

69 "The Future of Politics", three articles in *The Guardian*, January 8, 9 1968, the quotation coming from the first, "Bureaucrats in the Saddl

5/Seven Modern Concepts of Bureaucracy

1 Examples of this *tabula rasa* approach include G. Tullock's *The Polit Bureaucracy*, 1965, and A. Downs' "Theory of Bureaucracy", *Ame Economic Review*, Vol. 55, 1965.

Index

orussica, 52
istrative systems, comparison o
d and Coleman: *The Politics of eloping Areas*, 97
ur administration, 48
ism, anarchists, 36, 72
cracy, concept of, 17, 20, 31, 91,

tle, 20, 33
a-Hungary, 24
rity: Weber on, 39–45, 62–3, his eight principles of legal, 4
r, G. E., *The King's Servants*, 99

ot, 23–4, 30; *The English Con-tion*, 23
, H. P., *Industriebürokratie*, 98
in, Mikhail, 72
, Honoré de, 18, 30; *Les Em-és*, 18
B. H., 117
C., 60
J. M., *Our Wonderland of eaucracy*, 110–11
x, Reinhard, 57–8; *Higher Civil vants in American Society*, 57; *rk and Authority in Industry*,

s, 102
, M., 60
, insurrection (1848), 71
tein, Eduard, 73
rck, Prince Otto von, 47
e, J. S., 21
wood's 21
Peter, 58, 61, 90, 99; *Bureaucracy Modern Society*, 87; *Dynamics of reaucracy*, 58, 88; *Formal Organi-ions* (with Scott), 61, 87
eviks, 73, 78
, W. W., 114

Brecht, Arnold, 'How Bureaucracies Develop and Function', 93
Britain: budget, compromise over, 48; cabinet, 47; civil service, *q.v.*; political parties, 81–2 (*See also* England)
Brockhaus encyclopaedia, 28–9
Building industry, 59, 99
Buralist, 19
Bureaucracy: as administration by officials, 44–6, 98–100; as modern society, 102–5; as the organization, 100–2; as public administration, 94–8; as rule by officials, 91–4, 108, 122; concepts and meaning of, 13, 15, 18–21, 30–2, 50, 84–105, 120, 122–5; conservative attitude to, 81; continental theory of, 24, 26–32; democracy's relation to, 51, 103, 106–19; diagnosis of, 110–14; early definitions of, 17–18, 21; English theory of, 21–6; first academic analysis of, 29; four types of (M. Marx), 96; functions of, 24; ideological concepts of, 67*ff.*; limits imposed on, 47–9; Mosca's and Michels's concept of, 36–7; non-Western societies and, 60, 72–9; origin of term, 16–18; patrimonial type of, 96; rational bureaucracy, 43–5, 54–66, 87; remedies of, 114–19; term of abuse, 29; term in everyday speech, 124–5; two major types (Gouldner), 56; Weber's theories on, *see* Weber
Bureaucratic absolutism (Mosca), 34
Bureaucratic collectivism (Rizzi), 76
Bureaucratism, 29–30, 45–6
Bureaucratization, 104–5; Bendix on, 99; under Lenin, 74; Weber on, 45–6, 49
Bureaumania, 16
Bureau—or Einheitssystem, 27
Bureau system and bureaucracy, 27–9

Burnham, James, 103; *The Managerial Revolution*, 103
Bürokratismus and *Bürokratier*, 91
Business efficiency, contrast with bureaucracy, 24
Byzantine Empire, 41

Canadian Bureaucracy, The, 94
Carlyle, Thomas, 21
Caste bureaucracy, 96
Castro, Fidel, 78
Centralization, 100; de Tocqueville on, 30; Mosca on, 35
China: administration in, 16, 59, 96–7; bureaucracy, 23, 60; bureaucrat-capitalists attacked, 77; class structure, 93
Charles I, King, 99
Civil service: British, 25, 82, 95, 99, 110, 112–13, 115; German, 112, 116; Swiss, 99, 116
Cleveland, President, 23
Cole, Taylor, *The Canadian Bureaucracy*, 94; *Responsible Bureaucracy . . . the Swiss Civil Service* (with Friedrich), 99
Collegium, system of, 27–8, 44, 48, 50, 68–9
Collegiality, concept of (Weber), 47
Conservatism, 81
Constas, H., 59
Contemporary Review, 25
Conversationslexicon, 21
Corpuz, O. D., 57
Creel, H. G., 60
Crichel Down, 13
Crossman, Richard, *Planning for Freedom*, 82
Crozier, Michel, 90, 104; *The Bureaucratic Phenomenon*, 90
Cuba, 77–8

De Gournay, M., 16–17, 29, 31, 46
de Grimm, Baron, 16
Delaney, W., 59
Delegated legislation, 110–11
Democracy, 106–19; concept of, 17, 20, 31, 91, 103; conflict with public administration, 113; direct, 48; relation to bureaucracy, 51, 103, 106–19; representative, 48–9, 81–3, 118; Weber on, 46–7, 107
de Tocqueville, 30

Developing countries, administ and politics, 97
Dimock, Marshall, 89–90
Djilas, Milovan, 77–8, 92, 103 *New Class*, 77
Dorsey, J. T., 96
Dumont, René, 78

Eastern Europe, 60
Easton, David, 98
Efficiency: J. S. Mills' attitude t Weber's ideas on, 61–6, 88
Egypt, 41, 60
Eisenstadt, S. N., 15, 105; *Po Systems of Empires*, 96
Encyclopaedia of the Social Scienc
England: comparisons of admin tion, 23–4, 60; honorary publi vants, 35; local government parliamentary system, 49; patr bureaucracy in, 96; political pa 113; theory of democracy, 21–6 *also* Britain)
Etzioni, 101

Fascism, Fascists, 34, 67, 76, 7 94, 103
Feudal state, 34, 53
Finer, Herman, 92, 106, 109, 11 115
Fischel, Eduard, 33, 35; *Die Verfa Englands*, 24
France: bureaucracy in, 16–18, 3 71, 104; central administration educational system, 21; law relations of officials and citi 114; prefects' functions, 60; st movement, 78
Francis, R. G., 62, 87; *Service Procedure in Bureaucracy* (Stone), 56
Friedrich, Carl, 57, 60, 99–101, 1 111, 115–16, 118; *Respo Bureaucracy . . . the Swiss Service* (with Cole), 99; "S Observations on Weber's An of Bureaucracy", 60

Germany: bureaucracy in, 17–21, 32, 64, 66, 71, 79–80; *Bürokrat* and *Bürokratie*, 91; influence Weber, 50–4; Marx on Ge state, 68–70

s, Johan, 20–1; *Europe and the olution*, 20; *Germany and the olution*, 21
ner, Alvin, 59; *Patterns of Indus- l Bureaucracy*, 56
hay, *see* de Gournay
concepts of government, 17, 53,

m, Baron de, 16
ond, Jo, 82
diari bureaucracy, 96
skow, H., *Organisations* (with rch and Simon), 61
ara, Che, 78

y, Ferrel, 102
l, G. W. F., 31, 118; on powers of e state, 68–70; *The Philosophy of ght*, 68
elberg, 29
zen, Karl, 19, 28–9, 31, 70
ing, E. Pendelton, 81, 115; *Public dministration and the Public In- rest*, 118
art, Lord Chief Justice Gordon, 4–15; *The New Despotism*, 110–11
er, Adolf, 79–80, 112
ver Commission Report, 115
gary, rising (1956), 78
eman, C. S., 101, 111; *Bureau- racy in a Democracy*, 115

rnational Workingmen's Associa- ion, 72
y, *see* Fascists

ob, C. E., 118
nson, Dr Samuel, 21

nt, Immanuel, 18
plan, Abraham, *Power and Society* (with Lasswell), 93
utsky, Karl, 73, 78
ngsley, J. D., *Representative Bureau- racy*, 112
llontai, Alexandra, 74
aus, Christian, 18–19
onstadt, sailors' revolt, 74

a Palombara, J., *Bureaucracy and Political Development*, 59, 96–7
apenna, I., 77
aski, Harold, 92

Lasswell, Harold, 124; *Power and Society* (with Kaplan), 93
Legitimacy: belief in, 40, 43–4; conceptions of, 43
Lenin, 72–5; *The State and the Revolution*, 73, 75
Leonard, Peter, 88
Le Play, Frederic, 18, 30–1
Leroy-Beaulieu, Pierre, 30
Lichtheim, 78
Littré's dictionary, 18
Long, N. E., 118
Louis Bonaparte, 71
Luxemburg, Rosa, 73

Macchiavelli, Niccolo, 16
Managers and administrators, 121
Mannheim, Karl, 104
Mao Tse-tung, 77
March, J. G., *Organisations* (with Guetskow and Simon), 61
Marx, Karl, 34, 41, 67–79, 93, 113; attitude to bureaucracy, 31–2, 52, 68–72, 75–6, 103; criticism of Hegel, 68–9; influence on Weber, 50, 52; problems for successors of, 72–9; theory of the state, 70–1; works quoted: *Civil War in France*, 71; *Critique of the Gotha Programme*, 70; *Eighteenth Brumaire of Louis Bonaparte*, 71; *German Ideology*, 70–1; *Kritik des Hegelschen Staatsrecht*, 68–9, 71; *Manifesto of the Communist Party*, 70–1
Marx, Morstein, *The Administrative State*, 96
May Day Manifesto 1968, 78
Mayntz, Renate, 62
Medicare, 13
Mensheviks, 73, 78
Merit bureaucracy, 96
Merton, Robert, 15, 55–6, 58, 90; "Bureaucratic Structure and Personality", 55
Meynaud, Jean, *Technocracy*, 93
Michels, Robert, 31–2, 36–8, 42, 46, 80, 85, 94; 'iron law of oligarchy', 92; *Political Parties*, 36, 51
Mill, John Stuart, 22–4, 29, 31, 33, 35, 46, 66, 118, 124; *Considerations on Representative Government*, 22; *On* Liberty, 22; *Principles of Political Economy*, 22

Modern society, bureaucracy as, 102–5
Monarchy, concept of, 17, 31, 91, 103
Monocratic *v.* collegial administration, 50
Montague, F. C., *The Limits of Individual Liberty*, 25
Mosca, Gaetano, 31–9, 51, 85, 103; classification of governments, 33–6; concept of bureaucracy, 35–8, 42; plea for representative government, 35, 49; *The Ruling Class*, 33–4
Mouzelis, N., 62; *Organization and Bureaucracy*, 87
Muir, Ramsay, 55; "Bureaucracy in England", 26
Mussolini, Benito, 79–80, 94

Napoleon I, Emperor, 18–19, 27
Nazis, 79–80
Nettl, *Political Mobilization*, 87
New Deal, 13
New International, The, 76
New Left, 78, 82
Non-Western societies, 59
Northcote, Sir Stafford, 25

Office of Administrative Procedure proposed, 114
Officials: bureaucracy as administration by, 98–100, 106–8; bureaucracy as rule by, 91–4, 108, 122; control of, 114–15; functions of, in democratic state, 110–13; paradoxical position of, 32; recruitment of, 112–13, 117; Russian, 76; salaried, 32, 34–7, 53; social characteristics of, 55–7; Weber on, 41–5, 47, 58
Oligarchy, Michels on, 36–7
Olszewski, Josef, 30–1, 37, 45, 66
Ombudsman, 115
Organization: bureaucracy as the, 100–2; division of functions in, 55; modern, features of, 82, 121; principles of, 43–5; rational, bureaucracy as, 87–91; Weber's analysis of, 37–40, 100–1, 104
Organizational efficiency, bureaucracy as, 89–91

Paris: Commune (1871), 74; student revolt (1968), 78
Parsons, Talcott, 56; *Structu Process in Modern Societies*, 1
Patrimonial bureaucracy, 41, 5
Patronage bureaucracy, 96
Pipes, R., 59
Popular Encyclopaedia (1837), 2
Power: framework for study of, of public officials, 32, 110 separation of powers, 47–8; on, 39, 46–8
Presthus, R. V., 59, 101–2; *Organizational Society*, 104
Private enterprise, 81
Prussia, 19–20, 23, 27–8, 70– administrative system, 52, 54,
Public administration, bureaucra 94–8

Rational bureaucracy, concept of, 54–66, 87
Rationality: and efficiency, 62–5 90; formal, 63–6
Referenda (Michels's), 36
Renner, Karl, *Demokratie und eaukratie*, 98
Representative government, 48–9
Rheinische Merkur, 20
Riggs, Fred W., 96–7; *Administr in Developing Countries*, 97; "Ag and Industria . . .", 97
Rizzi, Bruno, 76–7, 92, 103; *Bureaucratisation du Monde*, 76
Rohmer, Friedrich, 28
Roman Empire, 41, 53
Rosenberg, Alfred, 80
Rourke, F. E., 113
Rules: attitudes to, 56–8, 116; Len use of, 73; Weber's, 63
Russia: bureaucracy in, 23; method administration, 59; revolutions, 60, 72–3; under Stalin and Trots 75–7

Sayre, W. S., 99, 118
Schachtman, Max, 76
Schmitt, Carl, 80
Schmoller, Gustav, 50, 52–4
Schumpeter, 82
Scott, W. Richard, *Formal Organiz tions* (with Blau), 61, 87
Selznick, Philip, 55–6
Separation of powers, 47–8
Sharp, W. R., 92

u-hai, 16
Herbert, 61, 65, 88, 101, 115; *inistrative Behavior*, 61; *Organi-ns* (with Guetskow and March),

, Rudolf, 57
sm: and Western democracy, lefinition of (Paris 1968), 78
scientists, working, 123–4
welfare services, 60
er, Herbert, 21, 25, 33, 35, 52
r, A. B. 60
, 74–5, 77–8
ed, 13
combe, A. L., 59, 99
, R. C., 62, 87; *Service and Pro-re in Bureaucracy* (with Francis),

ss, E., 89–90; *The Ruling Ser-ts*, 89
nt movement, 78, 118
n, H., "Bürokratie und Politi-e Machtbildung", 98–9
erland, 99
icalism (Michels), 36

Marshall, 77–8
sky, Leon, 75, 78; *The Revolution trayed*, 75–6
cey, coal industry in, 59

nployment procedures, 58
ed States: building industry, 59; reaucracy and administration, 23, , 96–7, 99, 110–13; central ad-inistration and control, 60, 115, 7–18; civil servants, 57–8; con-rvatism in, 81; Rizzi's opinion on, ; student movement, 78

Verband, Weber's concept of, 38
Vienna, 51, 64
Vietnam, 96
Von Humboldt, Wilhelm, *An Attempt to Determine the Limits of Effectiveness of the State*, 19
von Mises, Ludwig, 81
von Mohl, Robert, 29–31, 124
von Schulte, Friedrich, 24–5; "Bureaucracy and its Operation in Germany and Austria-Hungary", 24
von Stein, Lorenz, 19, 27, 29, 53

Warnotte, Daniel, 92
Weber, Alfred, 66
Weber, Max, 14, 27, 31–2, 37–67, 80, 84–7, 90, 99, 107, 113, 116; concept of bureaucracy, 40–54, 86–7, 98, 124; critics of, 54–66; his ideal rational type of bureaucracy, 43–5, 54–66, 87, 100; identifies bureaucracy with modern officialdom, 54; limits on bureaucracy, 45–9; major influences upon, 50–4; on administrative staff, 44–6; on authority and power, 39–49; on free parliaments, 48–9; "Parliament and Government in the Newly Organized Germany", 37, 47; theory of organization, 37–40, 100, 104; *Wirtschaft und Gesellschaft*, 37–8, 56
Weimar Republic, 80
Westminster Review, 21
Wittfogel, Karl, 72, 103; *Oriental Despotism*, 93
Woll, P., 118
Women's suffrage, 26

Yugoslavia, 77, 82

302.35